The Eclipse of a Smile

    A revealing story about an individual woman raised in the suburbs of the gracious south in a large family full of strong achievers, only to find herself a lonesome dove, amongst the pack of siblings, searching for a connection . . . and haunted by what she discovered.

## Acknowledgements

First, and foremost, I'd like to thank the one person who, without her words of wisdom, this book would not exist, Jennie Stephens. After I miraculously gave birth to my fourth and last baby, Jennie simply said, "You should write a book." Thus, *The Eclipse of a smile* was launched!

Next, I'd like to thank my loving husband, Mark, for supporting me like "The Rock of Gibraltar". He stopped at nothing to make sure that I had the best medical care possible, and he continued to search and pray for the healing answers to my dilemma. He provided me with full time help at the house with the children, so that I could stay in my natural environment and take care of the family.

Last, but not least, I'd like to thank friends and family who offered tremendous and unsolicited support and help. My sister, Diane, made family visits with my mom and dad, and she drove me to my doctor's appointments on several occasions. She also offered words of advice when I didn't know what I needed to hear.

Friends that came around and surprised me with lunch dates and visits to the LPGA at a local Country Club were Jean Hanger and Trish Brunner! The amazing thoughtfulness of these two friends who took the time and effort to express their love and kindness in this manner will forever be locked in my heart.

And to the "Great Oz", the wizard and master of healing, Dr. Noel T. Rivers-Bulkeley, I thank you with my life! As vibrantly and radiantly as the sun shines, so does my heart, and miraculously, also my mind! Thank you!

This book is dedicated to all who suffer in any capacity in this life, whether it is from illness, loss of a loved one, financial issues, family issues . . . anything.  Everyone can find hope in this story.

Chapter 1

The Early Days

It was a grey, overcast day in McDonough, Georgia on this particular autumn morn-in in October 1989 and quite typical for this time of year. It was now five months since the biggest event in my life had taken place. On May 20, 1989, my husband Mark, and I joyfully and somewhat wearily welcomed our first baby into the world. She was a very healthy and happy eight pounds, nine ounces and twenty-one inches long, little girl, named Jaclynn Cae Brittain (Jackie). Not only was Jackie considered to be a big baby by medical standards, she also proved to be quite large by my pint sized body type, as she entered the world via Cesarean section after seventeen long hours of unproductive labor. Jackie was my first introduction into the wonderful world of motherhood and the challenging escapades of morning sickness, light-headedness, nausea, swollen ankles and general fatigue. Although dreadful to endure these side effects of pregnancy, this first pregnancy was joyful from beginning to end.

To say that pregnancy and parenthood are two of the most mysterious and marvelous entities that this life has to offer, is putting it mildly. There are few words or sentiments to accurately express the full wonderment of it all. Now that Mark and I had the first few months of parenthood under our belts, it was time to venture onward into the next phase of child rearing as we began the merging process of the stay at home mom goes back to work syndrome. As most modern mothers would attest, this is no easy situation. The one time, all knowing, all powerful, young female who believed in combining a career with motherhood, now finds herself questioning her ideas and ideals on the entire matter. Nonetheless, since the decision had been made for me to go back into the career field, then it was time for me to prepare. Thus, I took my adorable, little bundle of love with me as I ventured out to run errands and collect items needed for my first day back on the job. On this particular day, Jackie and I were headed out for a regular romp at the mall for our girls' day out while I shopped for the necessary items that I needed. Of course, it's always essential to combine shopping with work related matter as often as possible. Since I was in the business of flying the friendly skies as a flight attendant (F/A) with a major Airline, it seemed fitting to bring the newest and cutest little flight attendant, Jackie, along with me. It was an ordinary day for the two of us as we headed out to accomplish our goals for the day. Jackie was snug in her car seat, and I was content listening to the music on the radio. As content as I felt at the time, I couldn't help but to be concerned about leaving the baby for the first time. I put on a happy face, but deep inside, I had actually been dreading my return to work. It was just so hard to picture myself stepping back onto an airplane, all alone, and leaving my little family behind. These thoughts had been bothering me for some time, but now that my departure was becoming imminent, I regretted the decision to go back. Balancing a flight attendant career and a new family is not always a welcomed lifestyle. The glamorous thrill of flying the friendly skies can't compete with the maternal bond of a new baby. Thus, my preparation procedures were drizzled with feelings of guilt, fear and loneliness. So, once again, today I would try to move on and push past my helpless feelings.

Now began my journey as I drove through the gray, omnipresent scene that hung in the air all around me that day. Despite my efforts to push past the encroaching gloom, I found myself succumbing to the negative presence of the heavy clouds that loomed overhead. The longer I drove, the darker the clouds became. The harder I tried to break the darkness, the deeper it sank into my conscious, and, before I knew what was happening, I found myself engulfed by a vacuum of doom. Panic and fear crackled throughout my body and mind leaving me frozen at the wheel of my Honda Accord. Somehow, I retained enough of my senses to realize that I needed to get off the road and compose my thoughts. Luckily, I found a quick spot to turn into, and I navigated the car back home.

Once I arrived home, I put Jackie down for a nap and tried to regain a sense of normalcy. I felt secure at the time because we were home, but I was still shaken by the experience that had so quickly taken control over me. As customary, in our house, if you needed to relax, then you poured yourself a glass of wine or some other concoction of your choice. So I followed through with a full-proof plan that would cure any problem. I poured a glass of wine and sat down to read a magazine. If Glamour Magazine didn't solve my problems, then I, indeed, would need to seek therapy beyond the rich and famous sporting the latest fashions that the Paris icons dictated to the rest of the world. Coincidentally, Mark called from the office to check on the baby and me. I told him about the strange experience that I had just encountered, and he seemed a bit concerned. He said that he would be home soon from work, and we would discuss the situation further then. Unknowingly, the episode that I experienced that day would mark my first encounter with a mental disorder that I had genetically inherited, and, yet, I never knew it existed. Thus, we embark on a journey into my world where I, unsuspectingly, lived with a genetically, inherited illness, and found myself confronted with it for the first time, only to discovered that the illness had long haunted my ancestors for years. In order to find a cure for the future, I had to first step back in time to my childhood which upon closer observation, I found, was riddled with symptoms of an unusual disorder, yet never diagnosed until many years later. Welcome to my world. Enter if you dare . . .

On August 14, 1962 when "the stars decided to get together and create something new" (Karen Carpenter, 1970), and obviously they knew what they were doing because, I was born! But I certainly wasn't a lone star because Mom and Dad, also known as Ann and Jack Cantrell, had a few siblings waiting for me at home; seven to be exact. I was child prodigy number eight, or so they thought. My parents didn't stop there. Eighteen months after I arrived on the scene, my brother Steve was born. He was the baby for a short while because a hurricane, named Leslie, was on the way. Two years later, the last page in the book of Cantrell's arrived with, yet, another little girl, named Paige.

Growing up, everyone knew the Cantrell's. How could you miss us? We were an indestructible force in the community being raised by a strong mother with an iron clad fist and a diplomatic father with heart of gold. Dad was a pilot for Delta Airlines, and Mom, the authority on raising children, was the head of the household. We grew up in the suburbs of Atlanta, Georgia; the home of Delta Airlines, Coca Cola, and the Atlanta Braves. I would tell people that I was born in a taxi cab between the Atlanta Airport and the Braves Stadium because Mom and Dad were at one place or the other. We were a rare species of people called natives of Atlanta Georgia.

I suppose that the reason my mother decided to create her own group of "village people" is due to the fact that she was raised an only child. Although, she had loving parents and a good home, she found herself alone much of the time. Raised in one of the more affluent neighborhoods in the Atlanta area, she was taught proper etiquette for a southern, young lady. She was always nicely dressed with a five inch bow in her hair that adorned all little girls of this generation. Apparently, during this era, the bow on all little girls had to be at least five inches long, so that each child could be accepted into the appropriate class of society. Nevertheless, my grandmother, Irene Holloway, made sure that, her precious daughter, Ann, was the "belle of the ball" everywhere she went. Later, as a teenager, she found great joy and contentment by simply walking to the neighborhood park and reading a book. Sweet, little innocent Ann also had her social click of friends, which were somewhat a mischievous little group. Their devious deeds were so mild compared to antics of our youth today. For example, their idea of being wild was to take an aspirin and drink a Coca Cola to get a high. Then they would play a game of truth or dare. Oh, those lost days of innocence!

However innocent darling, Ann was most of the time, she also had a rebellious tendency to her. Her relationship with her mother was somewhat strained at times. They were close, yet, distant due to many factors. My grandmother's father, J.M. George, was the Fulton County Solicitor at the courthouse in Atlanta. My grandmother also worked at the Fulton County Courthouse, and after she had Ann, she continued to work on a part time basis. Irene was a unique woman for those days, during the 1930's, because she had a family and a career. She also had a very active social life with my grandfather, James Roy Holloway. They attended many a gala at the Country Club, while Ann was left at home with her nanny. Through this lifestyle, my mother found the ability she needed to entertain herself. I believe she became dependant on herself to find her dreams and to follow them. I find that thread of self assurance in myself and in most of my siblings today.

To complicate matters for my mother was the fact that her father was a staunch Baptist and a strong disciplinarian. Therefore, any rebellious streak in her, usually met her at the front door with the porch lights on. She did try her best to challenge her father in all areas from religion to politics. Granddaddy, as we knew him, was raised in Flovilla Georgia, and made his living in the cotton business. Being that he was from a small town, he was grounded in a strong, Christian faith and believed in his deep southern roots. With the egotistical attitude of a teenager, my mother questioned her dad about God's existence. His response was, "If the story of Jesus Christ has been around for 2000 years, then there must be something to it." With that, she quickly changed her tune. Thus, it's with this strong independent spirit and a renewed faith in God that Ann ventured into her future. She met my dad, Jack Cantrell, at the ripe age of fourteen at a ballroom dancing class in downtown Atlanta. Dad was the instructor of the class, and the location was just across the street from the grand, Fabulous Fox Theater. They were quite a pair as they waltzed their way across the ballroom floor and eventually down the aisle to become one as man and wife.

Dad, also, was born and raised in Atlanta. He's the product of William and Clotille Cantrell. His history is not as well defined as my mother's because his parents divorced when he was just a little boy. Dad had one brother, named Harry, whom he loved and shared great times. During World War II (WWII), Harry's plane was shot down, and he was never heard from again. Dad claims that he was raised as a street kid on the alleys of Atlanta. His mother worked to support the family, and his grandmother helped to keep the boys. His upbringing was that of a survivor. He's told stories of playing in the street with Harry and other boys in the area. One day a rabid dog, foaming at the mouth, approached them, and they jumped on top of trash cans. Meanwhile, a police officer came around the corner, running with a Billy Club in his hand, and hit the dog on the top of the head. Dad said, "You should have seen the top of that dog's head after a lump grew straight up!" We've all laughed at that story ever since he told it! Life was always like that that for Dad. He always handled challenging situations without fear. His calm demeanor and reassuring courage have allowed him to accomplish great feats, such as earning the honorable position in the United States Navy, as an Observation Pilot, during WWII. Of course, upon completion of his service to our Country, he naturally continued his flying career with the, up and coming, commercial air line, Delta Airlines. It was during Dad's teenage years, that he developed his sincere desire to fly airplanes. He spent a great deal of time making model airplanes and flying them. Airplanes were his passion. On one occasion, the Atlanta newspaper wrote an article about Dad and his passion for airplanes at the early age of fourteen. Included with the article was a large sized picture of Dad with one of his airplanes. On the other side of town, there was a teenage girl admiring the article, and wishing she had the chance to fly. That young lady was Ann Elizabeth Holloway . . . my mother.

Since Dad was stationed in Pensacola, Florida during WWII, he and Mom married in a Baptist Church in Pensacola with a very simple ceremony. His job as an observation pilot was to guard the borders along the eastern coast of the United States. "I'm happy to report that no enemy aircraft made it past Tulsa, Oklahoma!" as reported by George Gobel (Johnny Carson Show, 1969). Back on the home front, during wartime, Mom was at home taking care of her two precious children, a boy named after Dad, Jack Moreland and a girl named Patricia Irene. They were affectingly known as Skippy and Patty. To this day, we don't let Jack know that we still call him Skippy, because he's a little sensitive about it. The Cantrell family was the picture perfect, all American family. The Royal Family of England never looked so good! They were the epitome of the *Ozzie and Harriet Show* for seven blessed years. After the golden years were over, and the war ended, then the equation of children at the Cantrell household began to change dramatically. Once Dad arrived safely home from the war, he delightfully settled into his career with Delta, and was stationed in Atlanta, Georgia. The union of Dad and Delta began a beautiful and successful relationship that lasted thirty years. Not only was Dad one of the early pioneers of the company, but he also exuded the traditional spirit of Delta which consisted of loyalty, integrity and ethical professionalism. These characteristics have been woven in the fabric of Delta's personality ever since it's inception during the 1930's. These character traits were also bred into my family's core value system creating a parallel and successful entity. Thus, my family life and the airline life were intertwined and sequentially grew together over the years.

Now that Dad had a secure position with Delta, it was time for Mom to fulfill her lifelong dream of creating a big family. So they got started. The beautiful, bright-eyed, Carol Ann (Candy) was born on March 23, 1955. Two years later, Susan Allen entered the world ready to help Mom and Dad keep up with the statistics of the Atlanta Braves score board. Just when Mom decided that she needed another smiling face to greet everyday, Diane Gay entered the world. At this point, Mom's doctor warned her against having any more children because her uterus was becoming too stretched out and wouldn't support another baby. Being the obedient person that she was, she got pregnant again. Only this time, she doubled her trouble with twins! Meet Carter Holloway and Karen Springfield. Meek and mild, Carter came first with his signature purple feet, and eleven minutes later, rambunctious, party girl, Karen bounced in! Of course, they were still striving for perfection, and that's when I appeared on the scene. I've been told that I was named after a beautiful woman that my parents knew, so they blessed me with the name, Connie Lynn. Eighteen months later, Mom delivered her first turkey on Thanksgiving Day by the name of Steven Scott. Of course, no family is complete without a hurricane in the mixture and that would explain the birth of Leslie Kay. Mom finally finished the last page in her book with a little girl named Ansley Paige.

Due to the constant and rapid growth of the family, we moved from house to house in the Atlanta area to accommodate the large group. After Steve was born, we moved into a neighborhood named, Briarcliff Woods, where we spent the majority of our upbringing. All the street names in the subdivision were labeled after cars, and therefore our address was at 2158 Eldorado Drive. We always thought that was a cool name to call home, and it's the address that we proudly called home for the next twenty-two years. Of course, our house was the house where all the action occurred, even though eventually we would not find ourselves to be the only big family in town. Back in the 1960's and 1970's people tended to have big families; not many had eleven, but they had five or six, which is big for today's standards.

Life in the big house was always fun and full of adventure. For those of you wondering how the daily operations of running such an awesome household were done, we can refer back to an article printed in the Atlanta Journal, summer 1966, titled, "Brood Cooks up Chaos" by Linda Bolt. According to this article, as stated by Mom, "Breakfast was served in shifts." The author revealed that during breakfast alone, we "consumed a dozen eggs, a pound of bacon, a loaf of bread and a never ending stream of milk." She also divulged that at the grocery store Mom would buy, "twenty pounds of ground round, fifteen chickens, twenty pounds of potatoes and four pounds of peanut butter per visit to the store." Another interesting query mentioned in the article was the issue of laundry. Apparently we did thirty-five loads of laundry per week. The laundry was placed in the chute, located on the second floor, where it plundered down three floors to reach the basement. Once the dirty clothes landed in the basement, our housekeeper, Carey May Brown (Cree) proceeded to tackle the enormous loads by placing the articles in the two washers and two dryers that we were fortunate enough to have. We called Carey, Cree, because the twins couldn't pronounce Carey. Not only was Cree the housekeeper, but she was also our Nanny. She wasn't like the typical, sweet nanny that most people envision. She was mean, and she kept us in line. Cree could put the fear of God into an atheist! Between her and our parents, we rarely ever got into any trouble. It was only the brave or stupid that even attempted to do anything wrong. Many attempts were made by some to reach outside the realm of the family rules, but Mom's wrath quickly dissolved any father occurrences. We were raised with a healthy dose of good old fashion discipline, and our content and happy lives today reflect the benefits of that upbringing.

Another point that the article stated was that the family stayed, "very healthy allowing no broken bones and only one injury requiring stitches." Many years later, only one other child required stitches, and that was me. Other than that, the record still stands today; no broken bones and only two sets of stitches! That's an amazing standard, especially in this day and age, where kids are easily breaking bones and heading to the emergency rooms at a consistent rate. Although, we do appear to have inherited healthy genes, the fact that we did drink milk during breakfast, lunch and dinner may have also improved our odds.

As we cruise down through the rest of the article, we find other interesting facts about the family, such as the family walking down the aisle of a Delta airplane on our way to vacation which caused noticeable reactions from other passengers. Another point made was that of my Mother's affection for writing and avionics. Her love of airplanes along with my Dad's affection for the industry has been genetically passed on to the kids. Skippy (Jack) has been flying his private plane for years and is currently involved in a programs called, Angels Flight, where they transport patients in need of chemotherapy, transplants and other related health necessities. Patty was a Stewardess, as they called them back then, with Southern Air lines and she married a pilot, by the name of Joe McArthur with that same airline. Candy married Steve Haynes, who attempted flight training in the United States Air Force, but was unable to complete the training due to eye problems. Diane married Steve Clinton, a physical education (PE) major at the University of Georgia, who later entered the United States Air force to receive pilot training. He also, landed a position with a major airline as a pilot.

As you can see, we had the typical lifestyle of the big family. Our story is very similar to the movie *Cheaper by the Dozen* in many ways. Several scenes in that movie are quite comparable to our family lifestyle. Some of the comparables are as simple as one sibling making the peanut butter sandwiches for the younger kids for school the next day. We made lunches, dinners, and we even gave out medicine to each other; including the over the counter drug, Novahistine, which now comes in prescription form! One of our all time favorite items to cook was green beans. Today, my brother in law, Allen Greer, thinks that we still have some serious issues when it comes to peas and any beans other than green beans Basically, we all knew how to take care of each other, and we learned to have confidence in everything we attempted to do.

Now that we've addressed the obvious operations of the family on the surface, we need to dig deeper into the family dynamics to witness the undercurrent of my personality and behavior in order to understand the beginning signs of a disorder. During my early childhood, my mother stated that I was quiet and shy. People that know me today would never believe that. According to my mother, I didn't start talking until I was five years old, and apparently my first sentence was more like a paragraph! The word out was that once Connie started talking, she didn't stop. That truth still lies within me even to this day. The reason for my quietness could be attributed to my curiosity about the world around me. I do remember questioning the human existence, and how we came to be. I wondered about how we got here and what our purpose was. I was more serious than the other children about life and its purpose. From my perspective, the other kids seemed to be "happy go lucky", and I always wished that I could be that way. It appeared to me, that the other kids could care less about life and the world around us. They were out to have a good time, and they seldom worried about anything. While they were living the care free life, I felt the need to understand certain events that would come about and figure out why they occurred the way that they did.

So here I am, this serious minded, young child living amongst a tribe of wild and adventurous thrill seekers! These differences between my siblings and me were actually the beginning signs of an on-coming condition that was headed my way. The condition is called Obsessive Compulsive Disorder (OCD). Apparently, that I inherited this condition from my mother's side of the family as we would later learn through my years of self discovery. OCD is caused by a lack of Serotonin in the brain. When the brain lacks the sufficient amount of this chemical, then it causes the nerve endings to miss fire as they connect messages to different areas of the brain. The symptoms that I suffered were that of excessive worry over things that most people would not even think about. I worried that just about everything that I came in contact with would somehow kill me. I believed that these disastrous events could only happen to me because I wasn't smart enough to understand how things in life worked. Everybody else, around me, seemed to go through life without these concerns, and that compounded my problem by making me feel inadequate.

My siblings and some of my friends noticed my symptoms and expressed concern about my behavior to my parents. My Dad gave me a pep talk one day about my situation, and he told me that if I didn't stop worrying, that I would get sick. Since, my worries were over getting sick, I decided that I had better stop. But, it wasn't that easy. Dad's talk did motivate me to do better, but it didn't completely stop the process. Later on, I would benefit from hormone changes in adolescence that would grant me a reprieve from the symptoms and allow me the freedom to enjoy high school. However, I had no idea that hormone changes were the reason that I was liberated from the condition. I thought that it was peer pressure during my high school years that allowed me to control my behavior. In fact, I gave myself considerable credit for tackling such a foe. Since my mind was free from the debilitating syndrome, I could explore the world of high school and set my mind on conquering the goals that I had set for myself.

As a child, we spent a great deal of time playing outside and learning skills from each other. So it was only natural for me to follow in my sisters' footsteps in athletics by competing on the gymnastics team for five years and cheerleading for four years! I made A's and B's in my academic classes and stayed on the honor roll for five years. I was one of the top five talent finalist in the Miss Lakeside Pageant my senior year. My future husband, Mark Brittain, who escorted the pageant winner, who also won the talent contest, said that "If I had asked him to escort me, then I would have won!" I quickly reminded him that I could accomplish my goals with or without him! Also, our gymnastics team won the State Championship for nine years in a row. Three of my sisters and I were contributors to this phenomenal effort. Susan, Diane and I all placed individually as State Champions throughout the nine year reign. Karen also received awards in her individual competitions, but her greatest accomplishments came from scheduling our "pig out" parties after competitions! Needless to say, I enjoyed incredible success as a teenager, and I relished in the thought of continuing that pattern with my goals for the future.

I began my college career at a local community college, called Dekalb Community College. It was an interesting start into the real world for a former high school cheerleader who was use to having fun on Friday and Saturday nights. Our football games were highly attended by the parents and fans of the winning team. After the game, everybody, who was anybody, attended the school dances. There was always a big crowd there, and we danced late into the night to the rock 'n roll bands that performed on stage in the high school gym. Life was a blast! Once I entered college, all that fun and frolicking came to an abrupt halt! On my Friday nights, I found myself studying biology for several hours. Needless to say, I had a lot of growing up to do during those college days.

After I completed my first two years, I finally decided that I wanted to major in physical education. It seemed a natural fit since I spent my entire life devoted to gymnastics and cheerleading. Also had two sisters, Susan and Diane that had majored in physical education while in college. With that goal in mind, I headed off to the University of Georgia to complete the task. I thoroughly enjoyed life on the big campus, but I was eager to get on with my future plans and graduate quickly. So I pushed onward taking extra hours and attending summer school in order to graduate on time. In June 1984, I reached my goals with a degree in Bachelor of Science in Education. Now, I was ready to roll!

Upon exiting the big university, I applied for many teaching jobs in the Atlanta area. The offers were few and far between. The only real offer that I had was a teaching position at a school far across town, three days a week, and the same position, at another school, two days a week. The schools were thirty miles apart from each other and my house. The job opportunities for PE teachers were limited, so I took a job teaching gymnastics at the Northside YMCA. I loved my job and the kids. After one year at the YMCA, I transferred over to another gymnastics gym by the name of Gym Elite. I taught there for a year, and then a career opportunity came about that I had never anticipated. A friend of mine, who was a PE Major at UGA with me, had been hired by Delta Airlines as a flight attendant. She said that I should give it a try. Thus, one month later, I was headed off for flight attendant training at Delta! And this is where I found a great passion for my new career. I had never before seen myself as a flight attendant, and now I couldn't see myself in any other profession. Traveling the friendly skies was always thrilling as was seeing the world! Those were some of the best times of my life!

A few years after settling into my new career, I started dating a friend of mine from high school. He was always one of my best friends, and I was anxious to see him again and talk about his accomplishments from the past and his plans for the future. He had recently graduated from law school at Sanford Law School in Birmingham, Alabama. He had moved back to the Atlanta area and had settled in with a law firm by the name of Smith and Welch, located in McDonough, Georgia. I was living in Alpharetta, Georgia at the time, so our dating commute was quite taxing. On our second date, the "love bird" flew in, and I fell in love. It amazed me that after all those years of dating guys from all over the country, I found "Mr. Right" living right next door! Mark Brittain and I had known each other for ten years, and it was during our high school years that we dated. To this day he still gives me a hard time because I wouldn't date him as a serious boyfriend during our high school years. I was too busy dating all the football players and other "jocks", so I didn't take him seriously. Plus, it's not natural to get serious with your best friend; or so I thought. Anyway, I finally had the fortitude to realize that my mother was right in telling my sisters and me that one of us needed to marry Mark Brittain. Six months later, on May 21, 1988, we sealed the long awaited deal with a ceremony and a kiss! And off we went to fulfill our dreams and create new memories.

As usual, with Mark and me, we tended to do things fast. And, so it was when we decided to start a family. Since I came from a big family, and Mark loved the idea of a big family, we were both ready to get started right away. After three months of marriage, we happily discovered that I was pregnant! Figuring out that I was pregnant wasn't easy. I experienced very bizarre symptoms that lead doctors to believe anything but pregnancy was possible. After many tests, including a blood test, we received the good news that not only was I not dying, but a new life was growing inside me. There's nothing quite like the feeling you get when you know for the first time that you are definitely expecting a baby. From the pink line in the window of the pregnancy test to the doctor's approval, we went forward with our plans to get ready for our new little arrival. Fortunately, I was able to take a leave from flying for the entire pregnancy, and then some, based on the type delivery that I had. Delta was very generous with their maternity leave policy, and few other companies offered as much. But, the maternity leave was very necessary for me because of excessive morning sickness. Of course, nobody tells you about the misnomer of morning sickness before the fact. You discover that reality all by yourself as you greet each day with nausea and weakness. And, of course, by now, I believe that most women have come to know that morning sickness is an all day and sometimes night affair! My husband thought that I had a more severe case than most women and wondered about how far we could realistically make it with our dreams of having a big family. Throughout the years, we have learned that although I did have my fair share of sickness, I wasn't as bad as other women. Despite the sickness, after a while, the glow of motherhood took over, and I tended to ignore the nausea and enjoy the pregnancy.

Once I reached five months, we decided to prepare the nursery. I had picked out the most positive and uplifting wall paper that had bright, multicolored balloons on it. On one particular Saturday afternoon, Mark's mother, Martha, drove down from her home in Decatur, Georgia to help Mark wallpaper the baby's room. I had to sit and watch, because a lot of movement made me queasy. So I sat enjoying the only sandwich edible to me, at the time, which was a baloney sandwich, while Mark and his mother worked away hanging the wallpaper. They laughed at my choice of food, and I laughed at their attempt to not kill each other during the hanging! After a long and laborious day of hanging the paper, Martha decided to spend the night and sleep in the baby's room. At 5:00AM she awoke to a strange crackling noise coming from within the room. She looked up and saw that the wallpaper, which she and Mark had so proudly hung on the walls, was unraveling right before her eyes! Mark's sister, Tammy, called later that morning to inform the two novices that they should have listened to her and properly prepped the walls before hanging the paper. I made another baloney sandwich, and watched, in much amusement, as they began the process all over.

Finally, the big day was encroaching upon us, as we waited with much anticipation. The closer we approached my due date, the more Mark wanted me to stay close to him incase I happened to go into labor early. One night, he had night court in another town, and he didn't feel comfortable leaving me at home alone while he was thirty minutes away. So, I got to ride along and join him for his night court duty. I thought night court was just a television show, so I laughed thinking that this was real court. It was the first time I had ever seen Mark work in a court setting, and I was fascinated by his performance. He showed a different and exciting side of him that I had never witnessed before as he aggressively verbalized his case against the opponent. I was surprised at how mentally tough he was and how articulately he presented his case. Markie Post from the television show, *Night Court* should be so proud.

Time marched on and so did the pregnancy. Back then, during the late eighties, doctors didn't mind letting women go two weeks past their due date as was the case with me. Not only did I go past my due date, but I pushed it to the max! I waited so long, that I started to forget that I was pregnant. One night, I got up to use the bathroom; once again, forgetting that I was pregnant, and I began to have some major "gas" pains! I thought if I could just pass this bubble of air, then I could go back to my blissful sleep. That blissful sleep has yet to return. The alleged gas pains that I had did eventually pass; they passed after seventeen hours of labor and a delivery in the form of a Cesarean section. But when I held the little person, who caused all my trouble, in my arms for the first time, I melted back into a loving, human being.

Since this event was my first experience with surgery, it took me a while to accept the fact that my body had just undergone a major and incapacitating procedure. During the recovery, immediately following the surgery, I began to actually feel a stinging sensation from the incision. I told the nurse about the pain, and she said, "Oh honey, you're not going to feel better for five days." I responded, "If I had to live another minute with this pain, then I won't make it five days!" Apparently, she had a bad bed side manner, and the pain medicine had tapered off leaving me in excruciating pain. After the doctor ordered some medicine to ease my symptoms, then I calmed down. In addition to the incident with the pain, I also, began to feel strangely abnormal in my conscious and emotional state. I can only describe the feeling as something close to an out-of-body experience. It was as if I was traveling into a foggy tunnel with no control over my feelings or thoughts. It was very scary, and very unpleasant. Later, when

I was out of recovery, I expressed my feelings to my mother, and she said, "You just had a baby; you're not supposed to feel normal." I just assumed she was right and chose to forget about it.

On day three of my hospital stay, I received my release papers from Dr. Schilling, and we finally checked out of the Henry General Hotel. We took the baby home in a flamboyant style by driving her in Mark's mother's, fire engine, red, 1975 Eldorado Cadillac that Mark and I had dated in. Once at home, we had a whole entourage of friends and family waiting for us and taping every bit of our arrival on camera. Jackie was the star, and Mark and I were the exuberant parents welcoming our baby girl home. Everyday, life was new and full of anticipation as we watched and admired every little thing that Jackie did. Once all the family and friends finished with their detail work of helping us out over the first few weeks, then we were on our own, and we set up housekeeping in our own style. Jackie would sleep pretty well during the night, and she would wake up at 6:00AM ready for a bottle and a change of diaper. After her morning feeding, she and I would cuddle up in bed together and get the best sleep ever. Mark trotted off to work at the office every morning while trying to establish himself as the new and upcoming lawyer at the law firm. And, so, life ensued in this blissful manner for many months.

As stated earlier, once Jackie reached five months old, and I was preparing to go back to work, the first signs of trouble began to brew within me. That gloomy day, where I experienced my first panic attack, set the stage for many unusual experiences to come. I did go back to flying, but it wasn't easy. As the days quickly passed and my return to work was becoming quite eminent, apprehension and dread filled my mind everyday. I would have given anything to stay home that first day back and never leave. The concerns that I had about leaving my new family created an overwhelming anxiety within me and contributed to the paralyzing effort I felt as I journeyed back out into the flying world. Mark thought that once I got back on the airplane and into the swing of things, that I would perk up to my upbeat personality and enjoy the art of my career as a flight attendant. He was mostly right on his assumption. After I entered the airplane for the first time in almost a year, part of me did get back in the grove. The difference was that it took a monumental effort for me to overcome the lugging feeling in my heart for my sweethearts back home. Most women that return to work after having a baby are gladly seeking refuge at the work place in order to flee from the family and get some rest. The contributing factors that played a role in my apprehension were that first, this was my first child, and secondly that my career was a bit unusual in the respect that I traveled for several days in a row. After a few months of flying and trying to adjust to my new role as mother and career girl, I continued to struggle with my anxiety. So, I decided to "ground" myself, and I applied for a position in the scheduling department. As flight attendants, we had the option to change departments from time to time. I was awarded the position that I wanted, and I began my new venture in the scheduling department in January 1990. Although I was thrilled at the thought of being on the ground, the scheduling office was not exactly the friendliest place to work. I felt like I had just walked into a lion's den of raging bulls. Apparently, schedulers frowned on F/As coming into their work space, but, I later learned they had good reason to act the way they did. F/As sometimes were quite rude to the schedulers, and sometimes made work difficult if not unbearable. What I was able to accomplish while I was there, was to bridge the gap between the two entities. The schedulers learned from me, and I learned from them. By the time my duty was up, I had made great friends with some terrific people, and our friendship remained throughout my career at Delta.

Well, after working in scheduling for two months, I was scared straight and ready to go back to flying in a big hurry. Working on the ground was definitely good for me, and I believe that it provided the necessary time for my hormones to get back to normal. I started back flying in March, 1990, and I absolutely loved returning to my first love. It was almost springtime and everything, including my mood, was blossoming. My happy and positive disposition came back, and I was off soaring with the eagles. Also, I fortunately developed a terrific schedule that afforded me Wednesdays and weekends off, allowing ample family time for Mark and me to enjoy with Jackie. The best part of this new schedule was that I would only be gone one night at a time, and I had weekends off. The pleasantries of life had returned for all of us, and we were now content to enjoy everyday and move forward with other opportunities.

Chapter Two

Trouble on the Horizon

Since I now knew the full realm of experiencing a C-section, I wasn't in a hurry to get pregnant again. I knew that I needed plenty of time to get over the birthing process, and I wondered if I would ever be ready to chance going through that again. One day, after visiting my sister, Diane, and her new baby, Amber, I felt the first twinge that I could, possibly see myself going in that direction again. Holding a new baby has that effect on a person especially a woman. Not only did I sense those old maternal stirring again, but I marveled at Diane's situation with her new baby. For several years Diane had been told by doctors that she was infertile. So she and her husband, Steve, tried all the modern, technical approaches that the fertility specialists had to offer, but none of them worked. After a while, Diane decided to give up on the treatments and leave things in God's hands. Once they decided to stop the treatments, and gave their plight to God, then he, in return, gave them a beautiful baby girl! God does work in mysterious ways. To everyone's surprise, later Diane and Steve would again meet with an unexpected fate.

After holding Amber as a newborn, and realizing that I could go through another pregnancy and courageously face the strong possibility of enduring another c-section, my subconscious began to work on the idea. In July 1990, I informed Mark that September would be a good time for us to start trying for baby number two. According to my compilations, September was the perfect opportunity to get started, but as God would have it, plans for another baby were already underway.

By the end of July, my plans for a September starting date were quickly altered by the presence of that, old familiar and barely visible, pink line that revealed itself after I took a pregnancy test. I don't know what made me thing that I could plan a pregnancy date or any other monumental event in my life. I've never had any real control over any part of my life, so I don't know what made me think that planning a pregnancy would be any different. I've also noticed that when God wants me to reproduce, he allows my brain to turn into mush. Every time that Mark and I have conceived a baby, without trying, I have suddenly forgotten how to perform simple arithmetic and how to count days on the calendar. Before we know what's happened, we discover that not only are we expecting again, but that maybe we need a refresher course in math.

Once we confirmed my diagnosis at home with the doctor's tests at his office, then we made our announcement to our families and friends that baby Brittain number two would arrive in early April 1991. From there, we proceeded onward with our regular schedules including work and family obligations. Despite the possibility that my morning sickness could, once again, get the best of me, I decided to stay at work. I did last longer than I had on my first pregnancy. This time I stayed flying for a whole two weeks! The room service bill during my overnight stays was more than my paycheck, so we decided that it was time for me to take a leave.

The beauty behind this pregnancy, was that although, I did have some morning sickness, it wasn't nearly as debilitating as the sickness from my first pregnancy, and it ended at twelve weeks exactly. Another strange occurrence during this pregnancy was that I could now drink milk. Six months after I delivered Jackie, I became lactose intolerant, and I assume that this change occurred due to the changes in hormones during and after pregnancy. Hormones are constantly changing in women, and I've begun to accept that everything is "fair in love and war" and . . . hormones. Fortunately, everything went very smooth with this pregnancy, and I felt great most of the time. I completely enjoyed my time off with Jackie as we played and took walks around the neighborhood. One concerning factor during this jubilant time was the ongoing Gulf War which had just started in August, 1990. Not only were we perplexed as we sat staring at the television watching bombs go off in the night sky over Iran, we also marveled about the chaos in the world which lead to this disturbing set of events. Mark and I were raised in a generation that was "happy go lucky" and familiar with good times and easy life styles. We hadn't seen or heard of war since we were babies, and we only remembered a few scenes from the television as it showed the soldiers coming home from Vietnam in the early 1970's. In conjunction with the present war situation, my doctor, Dr. John Schilling, MD, was in the army reserves and was shipped out to serve his duty. Fortunately for him and us, he made it all the way to

Augusta, Georgia; home to the world famous golf tournament known as the Masters Tournament. We relaxed somewhat knowing of his placement during this turbulent time for his safety as well as ours. Fortunately, Dr. Schilling was allowed to travel home to McDonough on the weekends and deliver babies when he was on call. We were thrilled with this concept because we had so much confidence in him after he delivered Jackie. Throughout the pregnancy, I would see a new doctor in Dr. Schilling's practice by the name of Dr. Shoba Rani, MD. Not only was she smart and sophisticated, she was beautiful! I enjoyed seeing her and learning all about her during my office visits. One time, Dr. Rani didn't realize the eruption of mayhem that could occur in the office when I was placed in one room, and my best friend, Susie Grant, who was expecting twins, was located in the room next to mine. An expectant mother with twins is enough double trouble, but combining that situation with another, wild and crazy, expectant mother, and you've got combustible chaos. Susie and I only hoped that Dr. Rani would make it through the appointments and promise to still deliver our babies despite our antics that day.

As the time moved on, so did the pregnancy and I kept busy with Jackie and preparing the house for the new arrival. Jackie helped me host our first, ever garage sale. While she took naps, I would gather as many unneeded items from our basement and haul them via Jackie's stroller through our back yard and into the garage. This routine provided an enormous workout for me, and probably more than I should have done. However, with that thought in mind, I plunged onward with relentless determination to prepare the nest for the upcoming arrival. There's something unique and anonymous about maternal nature, whether human or animal, and the fortified capability it has to produce, cultivate and protect its offspring.

Later on, after Jackie finished her nap, she would join me in labeling the items to sell with price tags, which provided great joy for young, sticky fingers, kind of kid. She and I worked hard and finally completed our task just in time for the big sale day. Interestingly, the day before the garage sale, somebody informed me that placing an ad in the newspaper to advertise a garage sale, can also alert perspective thieves to shop early leaving the seller empty handed. Ironically, the night before the sale, as we slept, I awoke to an obvious noise coming from the basement below! I lay still waiting to determine exactly what the noise was and from where it originated. Of course, Mark continued to sleep throughout the whole thing not wincing once. As I waited, I heard the noise again, and it was loud enough for me to know without a doubt that someone was in the basement stealing our stuff! For whatever reason, amazingly, I did not panic or call the police. I did try to wake Mark up, but he was oblivious. I decided that if the thieves wanted our things that badly, then they could have them. The idea was to get rid of junk that we didn't need anyway. As I stated earlier, we did move most of the items to the garage, but we still had a few things left in the basement. I figured that the thieves had probably already taken everything from the garage, and now they were now finishing off the basement. It marvels me that I could be so pregnant and calm at the same time. Once the noises stopped, I just, gently, drifted off to sleep.

The next morning as I awoke, I had actually forgotten all about the previous night's incident until I heard Mark up and moving around in the den. I thought to myself, I can't wait to tell him what happened last night! I just knew that once we opened the garage door, that we would see everything gone from sight. As I entered the den, I announced to Mark the events of the past several hours, and he said, "Everything is fine in the garage." I couldn't believe his words! I exclaimed, "No way!" Then I proceeded to inform him of the strange and obvious noises that I had heard coming from the basement during the night! He was perplexed about my story and slightly amused since unusual happenings tend to come my way. With my bizarre story hanging in the air, we decided to check the basement. Every-thing was just as we had left it. Okay, so now Mark did believe that my hormones were going a little wacky. We proceeded on with the day and had a wonderful time selling everything to all the customers that showed up. We ridded ourselves of everything and nested a nice amount of cash from our sales. Later on that night, Jackie stayed home with a sitter, and Mark and I enjoyed a nice, celebratory dinner at the Red Lobster.

As we retired for the evening, I again awoke to the same sounds that I had heard the night before. This time, I insisted that Mark wake up, so that he could hear the noises also. Thankfully, he did awake, and he did hear the same clatter! Halleluiah, I wasn't going crazy; not yet anyway! Mark wasn't startled by the racket that continued below us either, just as I hadn't been the night before. We decided to sleep on it, and determine the cause of it all in the morning. The very next morning, Mark approached the basement only to find a curious possum lurking about the basement! Armed with a broom, Mark bravely and brainlessly, decided to engage in warfare with the wildlife creature by heroically persuading the animal out of the basement via the broom! Mark actually could not believe that the possum became enraged and ferocious at him while under attack. Eventually, Mark was successful in his strategy to place the animal back into his natural habitat, and thankfully, neither he nor the possum was harmed. I later told Mark that I could not believe that he went after a possum with a broom, cornered the possum, and didn't expect the possum to retaliate with a possible, rabid bite for him. Needless to say, we had a successful garage sale, we caught our basement caper, and we enjoyed a great, big laugh!

Now that the house was cleaned out, I was more relaxed about my impending due date. Knowing what a "neat freak" I am, I probably overdid things little because I went into labor early. While grocery shopping at our local grocery store name, Zack's, I started feeling very strong contractions around my stomach indicating the onset of labor. My due date was only two weeks away, so I wasn't startled by this new revelation. However, I was pleasantly surprised at the initial contractions, since I had gone over my due date by two weeks with Jackie. Upon reaching home, I told Mark about the contractions, and we decided to ship Jackie off to the sitters, Fred and Shirley Rainer, who were fantastic fun friends of ours. They were also experts on raising children as they had already successfully raised their own kids. The decision to transfer Jackie over to the Rainer's so early into the perceived labor, was because it was late in the evening, and we didn't want to call Fred and Shirley in the middle of the night if my labor continued. At the time we thought that was the best for everybody involved.

My contractions continued to strengthen, and they stayed consistent to the point that Mark and I felt that it was time for us to head over to the hospital. Fortunately, we lived close to Henry General, so we never had to worry about traffic or distance problems getting in the way. Once at the hospital, the staff admitted me and gave me a room, a hospital gown and the whole works. They called the doctor who was on call that night which was Dr. Rani. She told the nurses that she would soon be in to check me and determine my progress. Everything was calm, and I relaxed in my bed while the contractions kept their own rhythmical beat throughout the night. Even though the contractions were still strong, they were not bothersome at all. Mark was escorted to the lobby where he eventually fell asleep on the sofa. At about three o'clock in the morning, as I lay on my back, I noticed that the contractions had stopped. By morning time, a nurse came in and told me that since my contractions had stopped, then it indicated that I was in false labor. Mark was a bit ruffled that Dr. Rani didn't come in during the night, as she had stated she would, to check on me, which would have let us know that this was false labor. To this day, he still complains about being left on the hospital sofa all night long to sleep when he could have enjoyed a good night's rest at home. I still have to remind him that sleeping on a hospital sofa is nothing compared to enduring labor at any given time! Well, Dr. Rani did come in that morning to check on me, and she dismissed me stating that the baby wasn't ready yet. We left the hospital and drove home to recollect ourselves and prepare again for the real labor. Mark's sister, Tammy, met Fred and Shirley at Mark's office to hand Jackie over to her for the rest of the week. Tammy thought that would be better for everyone concerned in case I went into labor again before the week was out. The false labor began on Tuesday, and on Thursday I was to follow up with Dr. Rani for a regular appointment. On Thursday I had a great visit with Dr. Rani, and she predicted that I would deliver before the following week's appointment. Upon leaving her office, I joined Mark for lunch to celebrate his birthday. He was turning twenty-nine on this day, and we were just beginning our celebrations for him. I was also, flying high on cloud nine while contemplating the impending birth of a new baby and relishing in Jackie's safe placement at Aunt Tammy's home. I've learned that when these moments come along, it's imperative to fully embrace them as they can sometimes be few and far between. As well as everything was going, it was ironic that the minute I walked out of the restaurant with Mark, I felt the beginnings of a fever come over me. I was too happy to be concerned about my symptoms, so I just took Tylenol and continued on my merry way. Apparently, I had picked up a virus from Jackie that she had had the previous weekend. She had no other symptoms other than a fever, and it lasted for about twenty four hours. Nonetheless, I wasn't concerned. As the afternoon past, I began to feel a little weak from the fever, but I was determined to make dinner that night with Mark and his family for his birthday! One of the topics that we talked about that night at dinner was what would happen to the Social Security Agency if the baby was a boy, who we would name after Mark, and was born on Mark's birthday? We had a great time discussing that story and sharing other family stories that night at dinner, and I felt that my effort was well worth it. Now, my goal was to increase fluids and get rid of the fever before I went into labor.

On our way home, we stopped at our friend's house quickly to say hello and update them on the week's events. I told them that the only obstacle in the way of delivery was the fever, but that I would get it under control. I had enough sense to realize that labor riddled with a fever was not a good combination. We drove home and readied ourselves for a good night's sleep. We both slept beautifully throughout the night, and Mark left for the office at his usual time. I stayed in bed and slept a little longer and enjoyed a restful morning. However, the minute my feet hit the floor, the contractions started up again. I had continued to have irregular contractions all week, so I decided to just wait and see if these would develop into anything. After talking to my amusing and crazy, compadre, Susie Grant, on the phone, the contractions seemed to take on a whole new dimension. It was just past eleven o'clock in the morning, and I began to notice a pattern with the contractions. As I monitored the pattern, the contractions became much stronger, quickly. I called the doctor's office, and they told me to come in for a check. Then, I called Mark at the office to tell him to me to pick me up, and he actually asked me if I could drive myself to the doctor's office. I know that for some women this may not be a big deal, but for me, it was incomprehensible. My theory was that labor pains are unpredictable, and so is a pregnant woman driving under the influence of labor. Needless to say, Mark picked me up, and he drove us to Dr. Rani's office to determine if I was truly in labor this time. Well, something was going in the right direction, because Dr. Rani did confirm that I was in labor, and she admitted me to the hospital. Due to all the excitement, I totally forgot to tell her about the fever. Since the Tylenol was doing such a good job taking down the fever, I had forgotten all about it. I was just focused on having a baby! Once we arrived at the hospital, we checked in with the mindset that this time we were definitely having a baby, and it was all systems go! I was hoping that I could deliver the baby via a process called Vaginal Birth after a Cesarean (VBAC). As I have stated before, I'm not crazy about surgery. Not only that, but I'm a very competitive person who believes that I should be able to do what Mother Nature intended. With those ideals in mind, we set our goals for the day.

As we began settling in the hospital, Mark proceeded to the car to retrieve the necessary items that I would need including the video camera. As he entered the elevator, he met Dr. Schilling returning from Army Reserves for his weekend duty at Henry General. Mark said, "I guess you know why we're here?" And Dr. Schilling replied in his usual, calm demeanor, "No, what's going on?" Once Mark informed him of my condition, he was ready to take charge. Although, I had failed to tell the other doctor about the fever, once Dr. Schilling entered the room, he took one look at the monitor and asked me, "Do you have a fever?" I was so surprised that he figured that out without ever asking me one question. At that point, he decided that it was necessary to perform a test on the baby to allow us to know how hot the baby's temperature was. He explained that since a baby is enclosed in a sac of fluid, then there is no way for heat to escape the heat, thus allowing the baby's body to reach temperatures that can be very dangerous. If the heat continues for too long, serious problems can result. After he performed the test, he determined that an emergency C-section was imminent. So, once again, the wheels were in motion for surgery, and VBAC was out of the question. I was a little disappointed, but ready to get the baby here safely.

In the operating room, I heard the familiar sounds of preparation and all the "bells and whistles" that accompany such surgery. One sound that I heard that I wasn't familiar with was that of the anesthesiologist calmly, yet, urgently telling everyone that we needed to get a cold mat under the mom because my fever had spiked to over one hundred and five degrees! He had an Indian accent as he spoke to me he said, "Nobody tell me you have fever!" After the cool mat was placed under me, I do remember watching the screen with the digital numbers indicating that the fever was, indeed, coming down quickly. I never panicked because I didn't feel much different, and I didn't really have a choice in the matter. From that point on, everything proceeded as normally as possible. As with my previous C-section, I began to feel the gentle tugging in my abdomen indicating imminent birth of the baby. Obviously, I waited with great anticipation for the arrival of the baby and the ensuing cries that would gleefully fill the operating room upon the baby's first breath. As I laid on the operating table, patiently waiting for the imminent birth, I remained somewhat perplexed by the quietness of the surgery room. People were still working on me, and the tugging sensation in my abdomen had ceased indicating that the baby most likely had arrived. Someone in the room announced, "It's a girl!" At this point, I usually cry along with the baby as I hear that first utterance of life stem from her tiny body, but in this case, the compulsion to vent my tears never emerged. I asked, out loud, "Is she okay?" Dr. Schilling simply said, "She's just a little sleepy." One of the many reasons that I didn't panic at this time is because someone had recently told me a story of their child's birth, and professed that the baby did not make a sound at birth. He stated that his son never made a peep, and that he just looked around the room out of curiosity. Equipped with this knowledge, I remained calm and felt that silence wasn't necessarily a bad thing. Although the hushed ambiance of the room was somewhat daunting, I knew better that to jump to conclusions and assume the worst. Unruffled by the confusion of the situation, I chose to stay calm and composed while thinking that everything would most likely turn out fine. Begrudgingly, Mark was taping the entire delivery on our video camera as I had asked him to do, so that I could enjoy revisiting those precious moments over the years. He stopped taping when he realized that there was a problem with the baby. Thankfully, he did get the important parts of the delivery on camera, so that I could later view the tape and understand what had happened to the baby. One such incident that Mark was able to record was the Pediatrician, Dr. Clifford Kauffman saying to the baby, "Breathe baby, breathe." That specific scene would probably bother most parents, but, for me, it provided a wealth of information to help me comprehend the trouble that the baby had encountered. I'm a person of great detail, and I need complete descriptions with stories and events in order to fully comprehend the outcome of such stories. Mark is the exact opposite. Ironically, for or a lawyer, he gets as brief as he can with details about events when he's talking to me. It absolutely drives me crazy! For example, when any of the wives of the lawyers, or any of the female lawyers within the firm, gives birth, Mark will usually inform me about the event several weeks after the baby has been born. When I ask him simple, specifics about the baby, he has no knowledge. He doesn't remember the sex of the baby or the name of the baby. He's useless in this arena. Therefore, I have to go to great measures in order to obtain the information that my inquiring mind needs.

As the medical team continued to work on Jamilynn Ann Brittain, Dr. Schilling continued to finish up his work on me. After I was sewed up and put back together, I was rolled into the ever-lovely recovery room where fear of death and dying looms a little too closely. Upon my entry into the recovery room, the drug induced haze of confusion began to set in my mind. As my mind began floating into oblivion, and my body drifted toward the Twilight Zone, I was dumbfounded to realize that I actually overheard the nurses ordering *pizza* for dinner! I thought, *what's this?* I'm questioning my chances of survival at this present time, and these women are ordering pizza! Oh, wait a minute . . . how could I forget . . . it's Friday night! Of course, it's Friday night! Order pizza, order margaritas! Let's have a party! And, by the way, could somebody tell me how my daughter is doing? Finally, I noticed the sound of familiar footsteps coming towards me, and it was Dr. Schilling. He had come to tell me the news about Jamie. As I suspected, there were problems in the delivery room, and all was not well with the baby. Dr. Schilling proceeded to tell me that Jamie was experiencing some respiratory problems, and that she would need to be sent to Egelston Children's Hospital. I handled the news well, especially since I was drugged at the time. All I could think about was that I needed to get well, and get well quickly in order to take care of my new baby. I didn't even know if I was sick, but I did know that I wasn't feeling well. I guess that a virus, a high fever and surgery constitutes good reasons to feel poorly. However bad I felt, I didn't have time to worry about my condition. I was determined to get over my hurdles and move on to taking care of Jamie and getting her up to par!

After recovery was over, I was moved to a regular room on the maternity floor. It was at this time that I began to regain full consciousness and communicate with everyone more coherently. Despite all the trauma of the day, we did have some room for humor which is often the case. During the course of confusion, there was talk among all interested parties that the baby would possibly need to be taken to Egelston by helicopter. Listening to my mother-in-law and my husband decide which of the two of them would ride in the helicopter was hilarious! I could just see the headlines, "Granny Flies High to Save Baby." As it turned out, there was never a need for a helicopter or any extra passengers to help escort the baby to her new destination. Jamie would do just fine riding in the ambulance, properly named, *Angle Two*, and she would be cared for by the paramedics only. The paramedics brought little Jamie in to see me before they took her off. She was encapsulated in her little incubator, with a fair amount of tubes and apparatus connected to her along with an oxygen mask. She actually looked very healthy for a sick, baby. Since she was a full term baby, she was a good size weighing in at seven pounds and twelve ounces. This was only the second time that I had seen Jamie and the visit was brief since the paramedics were anxious to get her off to Egelston. Once again, I stayed calm because my philosophy is that if I can't control what's going on, then I know to pray and let God do his work. I only worry about things that are under my control in which I need to act and failure to do so could cause a problem. Fortunately, for me, having put my life and faith in God's hands, ultimately I know that things will work out for good. Besides that, everything in life is under God's control, and we need to relinquish all things to him.

After Jamie was safely sent off to her new, temporary home, all of my concerned visitors started to disperse and headed home for the evening. Mark made sure that I was settled in comfortably before he left to get some well deserved rest. Eventually, I finally drifted off to a sound sleep and slept well until the phone rang at 1:00AM. As I answered, the pediatric doctor from Egelston, Dr. Kathryn Hudson, greeted me on the other end. She was incredibly sympathetic about the disturbing set of circumstances surrounding the birth of Jamie and reassuringly optimistic about Jamie's ability to recover. She was completely baffled at the whole ordeal because she couldn't find the exact cause of the problem. According to her, the doctors at Henry Medical, started antibiotics on me during the delivery process allowing the medicine to reach the baby. Once the antibiotics reached Jamie, they started fighting the infection; therefore, the infection did not show up on any of the lab tests that were performed on Jamie. This reasoning, lead me to the hope that Jamie would most likely progress to full recovery without any further setbacks. The concern at this time was for Jamie to get the necessary oxygen that she desperately needed along with the proper fluids. The hope was that, as the days past, that Jamie would need less oxygen. Once she could wean off the oxygen, then all she had to do was finish the round of antibiotics, and then be released to go home. That was the outlook from that first night, and thankfully, that plan came to fruition. As the days progressed, Jamie and I, both, continued to heal beautifully from our strenuous and difficult delivery. By the middle of the week, I felt strong enough to take a ride with Mark and visit her at Egelston. Recovering from a C-section is exhausting, so I was happy to have enough strength to step out a little and see my baby who was thirty miles away. Once we arrived at the hospital, I was placed in a wheelchair and Mark pushed me along the way to the floor where Jamie was located. As I approached her room, apparently she heard my voice and suddenly turned toward me. It was amazing to watch her automatically respond to the voice that she had heard from within the womb for the previous nine months. The nurse carefully disconnected Jamie from her bed and gently handed her to me. She was five days old, and I finally got to hold her for the first time. Once she was in my arms, she reached her hands up to touch my face. It was an incredible bonding moment for the both of us. Of course, in hindsight, she was probably trying to cover my mouth from talking so much. I was allowed to breast feed her, and she responded beautifully. It's remarkable to observe the natural response of a baby to be nursed especially after several days without her mother. Since I had never held her before, the bonding of that moment replenished my soul immensely. After the visit that day, Mark and I were optimistic that Jamie would continue to heal and that she would join us at home with her sister, Jackie, very soon. On day eight of her hospital journey, Jamie was released to come home and join the family. It was a day of celebration and great joy as our family was brought together to embrace our new, precious addition.

Once we were finally settled in our home with Jamie, life, for us, fell into place quite naturally. Jackie adored her little sister more than I had ever expected. I would put on a television show for the girls to watch, and Jackie would sit there and play with Jamie and tell her all about the story on the cartoon. Jamie would lay there and coo and smile back at Jackie in return. Whenever Jackie got the chance, she would change Jamie's diaper and wipe her bottom. Jackie loved to wipe that fanny! She would clean Jamie's bottom for twenty minutes making sure that she was squeaky clean. We caught these moments on video tape, so we have proof that Jamie did have the cleanest bottom in town! The two girls were constant pals from the very beginning, and we enjoyed watching them play and giggle with each other.

At six weeks postpartum, it was time for my check up with Dr. Schilling. I had been feeling great, and was confident in my abilities to run the household. During my appointment, we discussed my options for birth control, which was always a hot topic during this transitional time. Most moms, including myself, are eager to get started with a very confident form of birth control. I had problems in the past taking the birth control pill, but there was a new option, in the form of the pill, that was promising for me. Since Dr. Schilling was encouraged by the new revelations of this medication, then I was happy to get started with it. As luck would have it, if there is a side effect that no one has ever had with a new medicine, then leave it up to me to discover it. Yes, once again, I failed when it came to the newest, most advanced medicinal option of oral contraceptive. Yes, it's me, the human genie pig for modern, medical research! Let the "head case" begin because that's where I encountered my problems with the pill. All of a sudden, the tears started to flow and before I knew what was happening, my life started to unravel. I would cry over anything and everything. I was becoming sad all the time. I laugh about it now, but one day, on one particular incident, I became convinced that I would not live long enough to see my girls' weddings. When Mark came home, I revealed my insecurities to him, and he said, "Don't worry honey; I'm crying too, because I have to pay for their weddings!" He made me laugh for the moment, but later, my tears turned to obsessive worry and a great deal of anxiety. At that point, I discontinued taking the pill, and Mark and I met with Dr. Schilling to discuss my symptoms. Dr. Schilling was familiar with treating symptoms of mild depression for his patients, but my symptoms seemed a little more challenging than he had expected. He told us that my condition seemed more complicated than typical PPD, and he insisted that we follow up with a psychiatrist. I was grateful to him for admitting that this situation was beyond his control and out of his realm of treatment. From there we proceeded to find the right doctor. I don't remember how I found the first doctor, but he was a quack! He talked to me for all of five minutes, diagnosed me as having a nervous breakdown, and decided that I needed to be admitted to the mental hospital the very next day. When a vulnerable person, like me, at that time, needs help, it's easy to believe what a doctor says about you because you are so weak and frail at the time. It's hard for a person, in that predicament, to make a solid, objective decision. So, when I told Mark that the doctor was going to put me in the mental hospital the very next day, he went ballistic! He said, "No way; you don't belong there, and you're not going there!" I was so relieved at his reaction, because I didn't think that I had the courage to go through with it. Mark immediately got on the phone to a friend of his that was a psychology professor at Georgia State University. He talked with Paul Doverspike, who was a long time family friend of both Mark's family and my family. Paul suggested two Psychiatrists for us to call. Mark thanked him for his recommendation, and told him that we would follow up with him to see how I did. The very next day I called the first of the two doctors. Disappointingly, the first doctor was booked up with patients and couldn't take any more. I was loosing hope. Thankfully, on my next call, I received a welcomed response from the office of Dr. Noel T. Rivers-Bulkeley, M.D., (Dr.RB) of Atlanta's Mood Disorders Center. The receptionist, on the other end of the phone, told me that they had an opening. I was elated and relieved at the news. We set up my first appointment with Dr. RB which would become the beginning of a very long and fruitful relationship.

Upon my first encounter with Dr. RB, we exchanged very cordial conversation as he began to ask me questions about my past. After answering the many obvious questions that one would expect a psychiatrist to ask, it was quickly noted that I had never indulged in any recreational nor any "non- recreational" drugs of any kind, what so ever. I make a clear point about this topic because it can be quite obvious that a person with suspected chemical imbalances could have experienced with drugs at some point. Thanks to a great mom and dad who raised my siblings and me with much love and strong discipline, drugs were never a part of my vocabulary. I knew that if I tried cigarettes, drugs or alcohol that I would die from either the toxic chemicals in my body, or my parents would kill me. Either option was not worth trying. Also, during the interview, Dr. RB questioned my childhood and any strange behaviors that I might have had. I simply expressed that my childhood was perfectly normal, and that I was a very healthy child, "Except, I continued, during those years from the age of eight to twelve where I worried a lot and washed my hands constantly." Okay, back up here. Dr. RB offered, "Tell me more about those years." I explained that I was obsessed with the worry that everything in the world could and would kill me. I washed my hands until they were red with rashes on the top side. I further explained that my siblings knew all about my worry habits because I would confide in them, but I never told my parents. I also reveled that at the ripe, old age of thirteen, my symptoms seemed to disappear. As stated earlier I thought that the change occurred due to peer pressure, but as I found out thirty years later, the change actually came about due to the shift in hormones as I passed through adolescence. At the time, I didn't know why the changed happened, but I also didn't care. I was having the time of my life in high school, and I thought very little about my past predicament. I was happy, and I was moving forward with my career as a high school student, and I was enjoying getting involved with all the sports and activities that high school had to offer.

During this part of the interview with Dr. RB, I learned for the very first time, that my "worry habit" had a name, and it was called Obsessive Compulsive Disorder (OCD). This revelation was interesting and perplexing. I didn't quite know what to think about it. I came into this interview thinking that I had a mild, temporary condition simply caused by hormone changes due to child birth, and now I was learning that my childhood troubles were a strong link to my present day issue. It never occurred to me that I had a pre-existing condition that attributed to my current set of circumstances. I thought that I might just need some counseling or maybe a medicine, but it never occurred to me that I had a pre-existing medical condition. Growing up in my family, problems were seldom acknowledged, so, if you had an issue, then you needed to look in the mirror, point the finger at yourself, and adjust your attitude. Now, I found myself sitting at a doctor's office retrieving some foreign information from the doctor that I had not expected. He just diagnosed me with a medical illness. It made sense to me at the time, but it also perplexed me. While I sat on the couch in the doctor's office, and listened to him begin to tell the tale of my previous life, my thoughts wandered to the past . . . *so all these years of suffering and suffering in silence, and now it had a name.* I had a medical condition. My thoughts continued . . . *my mother quit driving a car many years ago because she thought that she came close to hitting a child one time, but she didn't.* I also remembered my grandmother, on my mother's side, would place a towel on a puppy dog in order to pet the puppy, and then she would pet the towel. My mother's father was bed-ridden from Parkinson's disease and suffered from depression. As a child, I simply thought that he was depressed because he was old and had Parkinson's disease. He was all of sixty years old, and he had depression so severe, that they had to perform shock treatments on him. He died shortly thereafter. Now, all these stories, from all the years were beginning to take on a whole new meaning to me. Pieces of the puzzle were all coming together, in one session, at the new doctor's office, in one afternoon. I questioned myself with all this new information. How could this be? I never knew. When, where and why? However strange it all seemed, at the time, it started to feel familiar. It became proverbial to me because there were hidden truths within all of it; recognizable because I remembered all too well what it felt like to suffer from the symptoms of OCD even though it didn't have a name back in the seventies; and memorable because of the constant fear that consumed my life and stole my freedom. Once again the familiarity of it all was becoming ever so present to me as I sat there on the sofa of the doctor's office remembering the stories of ancestors from days long past. Stories of relatives and their secret lives were locked away in the closet forever and scarcely told by anyone. My grandmother, My My, always talked to me about "ghosts in the closet." I knew she had something to tell, but she never would. She had many memories that she wanted kept in the past. I found it humorous every time she would start to tell me something, and then the story stopped with those "ghosts in the closet." I also remember, during my teenage and college years, when I would visit my grandmother, I would wonder and fearfully contemplate whether I would one day end up in a mental hospital. Back in those days, I never really thought that there was such a thing. I thought that if a person "cracked up", then they would end up in the so called, "Looney Bin." I knew that a mental institution was a horrible place to be, and, I, like most people, feared the idea of ever ending up there. I find it interesting, that at that young age, I felt susceptible to the possibility of my life going in that direction. As I now look back on my life, I realize that I must have had an intuitive knowledge, during those years, that my mind could be vulnerable. I suppose that truth had to come out at some point in my life, and now it had.

Once Mark and I finished our initial meeting with the doctor, he handed me some tests to take at home. He would complete the evaluation process after I had finished the take-home tests and after more conversations. Although we had just been dumped a "boat load" of information in only one session, we felt inspired that Dr .RB was definitely the best doctor for me, and that he would be able to successfully treat my symptoms. We proceeded home where I would complete the tests over the next few days. Once I finished the tests, we were anxious about the results. Surprisingly, to both Mark and me, I passed the tests with flying colors proving that I, indeed, was a normal person with a very sound mind. We were relieved and elated at the good news. With all that being said, we also had the knowledge that I truly inherited OCD, and that I would be more susceptible to anxiety and depression. My current diagnosis was that I was suffering from mild depression and anxiety. However mild the case may be, it deserved an antidepressant to rid me of the symptoms. So that's where we started with our first introduction to depression and its related disorders. Of course, we also thought that this would be the end of our troubles dealing in this new arena. Off we went, on our merry way, to continue our lives as we had originally planned, raising our children and tending to our careers. It sounded like a good game plan, but somehow, Mark and I always end up taking the path less traveled.

While waiting for the medicine to take effect, I started to experience elevated levels of anxiety that rattled my nerves and spun my thought process out of control. I remember, at one point, Mark and I went out to dinner with my parents in Destin, Florida. I don't even know how I made it to Destin in this fragile state of mind, but nonetheless I was there. Anyway, one evening, while we were seated to appetizers and cocktails (none for me) my head began to feel as if a rubber band was wrapping around my brain and tightening with every step of the process until my brain would explode. My thoughts raced along with the rubber band trying to keep up with the pace. And all this happened while I was just sitting there with my husband and family minding my own business! This is what it feels like to have anxiety. It comes on, out of the blue, tramples on your brain, and then vanishes like nothing ever happened. Nobody knew what I was experiencing at the time. I hid it well. It's always been my policy to "never let them see you sweat." The fact that these changes in my body could occur without any warning or any reason still baffles me to this day. It's all a foreign concept to me because I had never experienced anything like it before. It's bizarre, it's extraordinary, but it does happen, even to the unlikeliest of people, and I never thought that I would be a likely candidate.

Shortly after I began taking the antidepressant, I started to feel a gradual improvement in my mental state. It didn't happen overnight, and it wasn't a quick fix, but the medicine eventually became very effective for me. It took about a month for me to feel like myself again, and that was a much welcomed relief! You never realize how sick you are until you get a fresh chance to feel good again, and then its like somebody turned on the light into your life. The sun shines bright, and the flowers smell radiant again! Life was good, and I was happy to be alive!

While I was venturing into this new world, living under the influence of an antidepressant, I was also exploring a new opportunity at work that I had long awaited. The flight attendant Training Department at Delta was accepting applications for Instructor positions training new flight attendants. I had applied many months before, and my number came up. Instead of going back to work on the airplanes, I would begin a month of training to become a certified training instructor. I was elated about the opportunity and the affordability to try something new within the company. Since I had a strong background in teaching and a natural love for airplanes, this new title would be a perfect marriage. I was also excited about the fact that I would be on the ground and able to see my family everyday. Everything in life was starting to come back together for Mark and me, and we were happy to be sailing forward again.

Life at the training center was exciting, challenging and full of new prospects for the future. I enjoyed stepping out of my uniform for a while and dressing for the business world as well as learning more about the corporate side of Delta in an office setting. Meeting new faces and working with fellow F/As in a different arena was enriching. We all clung to each other as if we were kids at summer camp for the first time. We bonded very well and absorbed the new information and training skills that were necessary in order for us to become well groomed F/A instructors. As with most areas at Delta, there is a sense of family in every department. That family feeling goes a long way when it comes to accepting a new title in a new department. Everyone was gracious and treated us warmly.

Finally, as training was coming to an end, we each began to gradually move into our respective positions as instructors. Our training was coming to an end, so we started the transition from internship to the real deal during the final two weeks of training. I was one of the first ones to bite the bullet and try my hand at the first chance. I didn't have a lot of time to prepare to teach the airplane that I was assigned to teach, but I was ready and willing to take the opportunity. And so I did. Sometimes my mouth is bigger than my brain when it comes to taking that leap of faith. My knowledge of the Lockheed airplane that I was to teach was on par with the average F/A, however, my complete understanding of the intricate details of the L-1011 was not at a superior level yet. There was a lot of material to cover, and I thought I could handle it in the short period of time that I had to prepare. I knew that it was a gamble to take on this huge airplane with little preparation time, but I was always up for the challenge. About the time that I took off teaching the L-1011, I was ready for landing! I got most of the information right, but I also received "A Little Help From My Friends," (The Beatles, 1967). There was one student in my class who was renewing his F/A training because he had been in another department for a while. He had mostly flown the L-1011, so he was well versed with it and helped me out when I needed it. That was a pretty big responsibility for me to take on the first time up at bat, and I was embarrassed when I messed up, but I learned as I went along. My parents always taught me to take opportunities and give it my best shot. Life is a learning process, so go for it! After that teaching session, I began to get my groove on and teach my heart out. On one particular day, we had an official kick off day teaching the new Pan Am F/As that Delta had acquired in the latest merger. The head person of the training department was so excited about this new venture that she ran her speech overtime. I, of course, was the first instructor for the day, so it was up to me to teach the Boeing-727, completely, and in the short time frame of forty-five minutes as apposed to one hour and thirty minutes. It was time for me to prove myself, and I did it within the forty-five minutes, slam dunk, complete, and fully covering every aspect of the 727! I did receive a nice congratulations and pat on the back from the senior instructor in charge. Everybody was enthusiastic and ready for the next round! My fellow F/A trainees and I were on a roll and ready to fly solo! Off we went soaring to new heights in our new careers!

The flight attendants from Pan Am were gracious and wonderful people. Everyone in the Delta family welcomed our newest family members, and we enjoyed getting to know them as we trained them to the Delta Fleet. Most of our instruction in the early part of our training careers was to adapt the Pan Am F/As to the Delta system. We knew the merger was a good one with everybody working so well together. After we mainstreamed the Pan Am crews, we went back to teaching newly hired F/A's that Delta had recently interviewed and employed. Teaching the "new kids" on the block was thrilling for my fellow training classmates and me since we knew all too well how it felt to be a new member of this large company. We all remembered when we were in their seats, and we empathized with them immensely. The experience of teaching Pan Am and the new trainees was enlightening as everyday we met new faces and exchanged cultural information from all over the globe. There was never a boring day. Thus, my new title in the Delta Company was working out quite well for me, and I was glad for the opportunity. I decided that this was a good move for me, and I wanted to keep teaching throughout my career and alternate it with flying every so often. We flight attendants are restless birds. We have to keep flying or we'll get rusty. While working at the training center at Delta, I discovered a whole new world of opportunities available for me Delta, and that's where I set my plans. The sky was the limit.

I started working at the training center in July 1991. By the time fall rolled around I was well immersed in my responsibilities as an instructor. At home, Jackie was three and Jamie was seven months old. They were getting along fabulously well. Jackie adored her little sister, and it showed on Jamie's face. Mark was doing well at the law firm. The only problem he had was the constant flow of business at the office that kept him busy and preoccupied most of the time. But for him, that was a good thing. He's obviously very conscientious about his work which contributes to the amount of business that he was bringing in at the time. Times were good for us, and we were pleasantly enjoying the fruits of our labor. Did I say fruits of our labor? That sounds a little bit like a premonition. Well, apparently it was a premonition. I've decided that when God wants us to reproduce, he allows us to be stupid! All of a sudden, I miscalculate dates, forget what day of the week it is and totally misuse the latest device for birth control that the doctor has provided me. You can guess what comes next; it; another baby was on the way. I remember, one day, while I was teaching, I stepped forward toward the class to make a specific comment about an airplane, and the moment that I stepped forward, I felt a tug in my lower abdomen. I knew right, then and there, that I was pregnant. I had become quite familiar with certain body responses that pointed in the direction of pregnancy. It was remarkable that, with one swift movement, while performing my job, in the middle of the day, that I became cognizant of an impending pregnancy. A slight smile came over my face as I realized the news that I had just discovered about myself that no one else in the room new. From that day forward, other symptoms of pregnancy began to surface to the point that it was time to do a pregnancy test and see the doctor. Even though I do a pregnancy test at home, I always have another one done at the doctor's office to validate the pregnancy. Once we have that done, then we make the announcement to family and friends. We had to get this test done early because my eating habits were changing so fast that people would soon begin to notice. By the time we received the positive tests results from the doctor, I was only five weeks along. Apparently, I was learning quickly how to pick up on pregnancy symptoms earlier than I had in the past. After we had the confirmation from the doctor, I called Dr. RB to let him in on the news and to find out what to do about the medicine that I was presently taking. He told me to get off the medicine immediately, and to see him soon. He also said that I might feel a little strange as the medicine depleted from my body. A couple of days after getting off the medication, I experienced the strange sensation that Dr. RB had mentioned. I felt a little off kilter, and it made me a bit nervous, but it passed quickly. After that, I was feeling normal again.

We finally let our families in on our little secret just in time to keep others from questioning my ravenous eating binges. We told my parents about the news over the phone, but we presented the news to Mark's mother, Martha, and grandmother, Mamaw, with a little more style. Since Christmas was fast approaching, I found a Christmas picture frame in the shape of a train that would perfectly fit a picture of each of Martha's grandchildren with an extra window for the newest upcoming addition. We inserted all the grandchildren's pictures in each window, and we put my due date in the empty window. We had Martha and Mamaw open the gift together, and we stood back to watch their expressions. Martha stayed confused about the whole thing, but Mamaw caught on right away! Mark's eighty-year-old grandmother had to explain to her own daughter that the train picture frame held the secret to the future. They were elated, and they loved the technique that we used to give them the message.

After the news was out, we proceeded to adjust to our new set of circumstances. One of the first items on the list was for me to have an ultra-sound picture made of the baby at Dr. Schilling's office. It was early in the game to have an ultrasound performed, but I wasn't complaining. Every pregnant woman I've ever known looks forward to having an ultra-sound picture done, so she can actually see the image of the baby. The day arrived and I bounced right into the diagnostic room with the technician leading the way. The ultrasound tech set me up, and away we went searching the monitor for the small, white image. Dr. Schilling entered the room to observe first hand the third, baby Brittain that he would soon be delivering. As we all peered at the screen, we saw the white mass indicating the sac which envelopes the baby, but, to all of our surprise, there was no baby in the sac. I questioned Dr. Schilling, "Are you sure that there's not a baby in there?" He explained that it appeared to be a blighted ovum. That means that a sac formed, but not the baby. *Huh?* I thought. That's a new one for me. I asked him if it was just too early for the baby to show up since I was only five weeks along. He said, no, that I was actually seven weeks along, and that was far enough along for the baby to show up on the monitor. Along with his confirmation of the blighted ovum, he also decided to wait two more weeks, and then he would perform another ultra-sound to insure his findings. He informed me that I would most likely miscarry within the next two weeks. I left his office a bit stunned and dazed by confusion, but fully comprehending the situation for what it was. I drove straight to Mark's office to tell him the shocking news. He was taken aback by the news while he struggled to grasp the full meaning of this bizarre story. Bewildered by the news, Mark and I floated in a fog of mystifying wonderment for days on end, and at the same time, we tried to stay poised while we broke the news to our families. Upon telling my mother about the events of that day, she asked me how I felt about the situation. I told her, that honestly, we weren't expecting to have another baby so soon after having Jamie, especially knowing all the trouble I had after her delivery, so maybe this was a sign that my body still needed more time to recover after the last pregnancy. Maybe this was nature and God's way of taking care of me. As I've stated before, I don't worry about things that are out of my control. To me, this was clearly in God's hands, as all aspects of our lives are, whether we allow him to take control or not. So I was willing to accept the news to the best of my ability, and live life as normally as possible. From that point forward I anticipated a miscarriage at any moment, but it never happened. I kept looking for symptoms that I thought would be the trigger point at the onset of a miscarriage, but nothing ever materialized. I also knew that not suffering a miscarriage didn't necessarily guarantee me that the pregnancy could still be a viable one. If I didn't miscarry, then I could still have the same prognosis, but I would have to have a procedure called a dilation and curettage (D&C) to remove the non-productive tissue. So, here we were, waiting for the two weeks to pass until we could learn more about this awkward predicament that we were enduring.

The day finally arrived, and we anxiously arrived at the doctor's office and entered the ultra-sound room. We exchanged pleasantries with Dr. Schilling and the technician, and then they suited me up to the machine and began the scanning process with the magical wand of the ultra-sound probe. Glued to the monitor, everyone stared at the black and white screen nervously looking for a sign of life within white mass on the screen. And . . . there it was . . . a white mass . . . and . . . we all wondered, what else? A . . . figured appeared; two arms, two legs, a fully shaped body and constant movement from the baby as it swam furiously as if to say, "Put the knife away; I'm here!" We were all astonished, and Dr. Schilling stood paralyzed in amazement. There was the baby; dramatically stating to the entire world, here I am, here I am! According to my calculations on the date this baby was conceived, I truly believe that I was only five weeks along at the time of the first ultra-sound. Now that two weeks had passed, the baby had matured to the state of a seven week fetus and was visible with the ultra-sound. It just goes to show you that you can't fool Mother Nature! Anyway, we were all pleasantly surprised, relieved and grateful for the turn of events that ruled in our favor. It didn't occur to me until after the fact, but apparently, deep inside, I really wanted this pregnancy to work. Despite all the trouble I had after having Jamie, I felt compelled to embrace this pregnancy with full gusto and without any fear of any obstacles getting in my way. After all, God never gives you more than you can handle, and apparently, he believes in my abilities more than I do. Another advantage that we thought about was the fact that I might not necessarily endure the same problems that I had in the past, and if I did encounter any troubles, we now had a doctor and a medicine that could help. Mark and I tend to not dwell on the negative, and we strive to find the right answers when faced with challenge.

Now that we had good news to share with our family and friends, it was time to make some phone calls.

From this point on, we were able to move forward with no further complications, and I stayed on teaching at the training center until I was five months along. That was the longest stretch of time that I had ever worked while pregnant. Since I was working on the ground, it was much easier for me to keep going than it would have been if I were still flying. However, the morning sickness along with the early morning schedule, and the long days did take a toll on me, and finally, I had to give it up. I officially went out on maternity leave on March 1, 1992. And then the unexpected happened. . . .

On Saturday morning, March 21, 1992, I awoke early enough to make coffee and prepare breakfast before the little munchkins who got up early to watch their Saturday morning cartoons. Mark was recovering from a short bout with the stomach flu, so he stayed sleeping for some much needed rest. At 9:00AM the phone rang, and it was my sister, Leslie. She rarely called, and she asked for Mark. I was a little irritated because I thought she was calling for legal advice, early on a Saturday morning, when my husband was recovering from an illness. When I told her that he couldn't come to the phone because he was sick, then she asked me if I was sitting down. As I approached the chair to obey her command, my life started to flash before my eyes with the news that she was beginning to tell me. Before I could sit down, my thoughts were already trying to spin backward . . . backward to the previous, brief moments of the morning that started the day off with a fresh look at the world. The world that I knew as normal and happy was beginning to fade away as Leslie's words unveiled the story that would change our lives forever. My mind was racing backwards trying desperately to stop, her words from penetrating my soul. She was speaking of my brother-in-law, Steve Clinton, when she bluntly said, "Steve Clinton is dead!" (Even as I write these words now, my heart takes another piercing blow.) I couldn't fathom what she had said. I imagined this terrifically, beautiful man, larger that life, passing into the uncertain world of death. I questioned myself and Leslie, as to how could it is that this person, who lived and breathed among us, could leave this world? I persisted with more questions as I asked for the details of the situation such as where, when and how did this happen? As Leslie tried to explain the chain of events to me, all I could hear in my head was no, no and forever no! I couldn't take the news; it wasn't true; it couldn't be true. Steve was the strong one. He was supposed to take care of the rest of us when unexpected things like this happened. I began to hyperventilate as I tried to breathe and comprehend the news at the same time. thought about calling my doctor to get a medication to calm me down, but then I thought to myself, *no, you are stronger than this, and you will handle this!* I marched to the bedroom blasting at Mark to pick up the phone! In his foggy haze he followed my orders and picked up the phone to receive the unfortunate news; that one of his favorite people, in the whole world, had just died.

From that moment on, we tried to collect ourselves as we continued to inhale the unpleasant and unexpected news about Steve's untimely death. The hazy minutes turned into hours and hours into typical rituals of the ceremonious funeral and post funeral gatherings. My sister, Diane, held up well while in the company of family and friends, but time spent alone proved to be devastating. She has since revealed her darkest moments to us and described her pain as unbearable. Had her baby daughter, Amber, not been around, Diane may have lost her will to live. In past years, she has told us that she believes that God gave her Amber because he knew that he was taking Steve away. Diane believes that Amber is her saving grace and her consoling angel. The rest of the family also suffered its fair share of grief and desperation. At one point, just before the funeral started, the directors of the funeral guided the family into the room with the deceased to pay our last respects. I was standing next to my mom and I stated that this was difficult. Her response back to me, in her deep, compassionate manner, was, "Well, maybe you should leave the room." I, of course, was stunned at her response. I thought *this is where I'm supposed to be with these feelings!* I wasn't even crying or showing any emotion as I made my comment. I was just making conversation. But, then again, that's my family! The philosophy that we've learned to adopt is, "Never let them see you sweat" . . . or cry or show any emotion at all!

Once all the events surrounding Steve's death came to an end, the reality of getting back into the game of life proved quite difficult. The aftermath of any great loss is always the most challenging. After everybody leaves and there's no longer a support group in which to share your pain, a person can feel quite distraught. I was beginning to feel the agonizing turmoil within my mind as I tried to comprehend and relate to what had happened to Steve. Unbeknownst to me, Steve had been suffering from chest pains for the past six months. He grounded himself from flying as he sought help for his reoccurring chest pains with the doctor from the Federal Aviation Administration (FAA). He checked in with the doctor every month for testing about his continuing problem. Obviously, the doctor missed something very important! I'm not one to bash doctors at all, but this guy missed a big and obvious sign involving Steve's condition. During the investigation of Steve's death, it became clear that during one of Steve's stress tests, his blood pressure numbers were reversed. For example, instead of having a normal blood pressure of 120/80, Steve's was 80/120. Thus, a law suite did ensue, and my sister did win her case. Apparently, Steve was born with a heart condition that had gone undetected for years. To my knowledge it was not the obvious kind of defect that clearly defines itself. Steve had premature hardening of the arteries as the autopsy revealed an abnormal amount of blockages in his arteries for his age. Due to the abnormality his heart was greatly enlarged. He was only thirty-four years old and in top physical shape. He was a superb athlete all of his life, and during his high school years, he excelled in football as well as other sports. In college he continued with the same passion for fitness as he majored in physical education at the University of Georgia. As far as looks go, he literally had the looks of a movie star. People in Atlanta often confused him with Steve Barkowski (a former Atlanta Falcon quarterback) because he looked like him in size and stature. Steve was about six feet and four inches tall and chiseled from head to toe. Like I stated before, he appeared larger than life, and we loved him very much. Steve taught each of us lessons about life while he was here, and today, I still feel his presence in my life to this day. His daughter, Amber, is now sixteen years old, and she gracefully, exemplifies the strength and beauty of the legacy her father left behind.

Time marches on and so everyone tried to gather up the pieces of the broken hearts and move forward into the future. We did have many projects in the works such as my sister, Karen, and I due with babies just three months apart. She was expecting her first, and long awaited, baby in May, and, of course, my baby was due in August. Karen had been our mother's most challenging child to raise from the day she busted into the world with her debut at Piedmont Hospital in Atlanta, Georgia on March first, 1961. She was the second baby born of the twins on that incredible day, and she insisted on making a big splash! As I stated earlier, the first baby to arrive was a boy named Carter, but he never quite got in the spotlight because Karen was always overshadowing him. Carter's trademark when he was born was that he had purple feet which marveled the doctors and nurses alike. Karen's trademark was that she screamed profusely until she received acknowledgement from everyone on the maternity floor. She was the tomboy, the fighter, the antagonist and basically an overall little devil with the cutest, most angelic smile on her cunning, sweet face! Eventually, Mom and Dad had to put them in separate playpens to keep Karen from beating up on Carter. Karen didn't have much hair, and Carter did, so, she tried her best to pull out all of his hair out in order to make things even. Not only did she pull his hair, but she threw his toys out of the playpen and tortured him constantly. Carter never fussed about any of it; he just smiled like nothing bothered him. Later on, as they grew and became more mobile, Karen came up with new ways to give our Mother the nervous break down that she had always feared. One day while Mom and Dad were sitting out on the patio, trying to enjoy the late afternoon sun, they were bombarded with toys being flung out of a second story window! There are two reports of this story, so I'll give a glimpse of them both. Diane says that Karen had Carter hanging by his feet, and that he was throwing the toys out the window. But Mom has told me that she walked up the stairs and found Karen teetering on the window ledge throwing the toys out. Once Mom approached the second floor of the house and the room where Karen was positioned, she quietly motioned to Karen that she had some candy for her. With that incentive Karen quickly came scurrying back down, out of harms way, and into Mom's arms for a treat! The very next day, my Mom called a security company to put burglar bars on the upstairs windows. When the service man came out to the house, he called his boss and said, "Boss, you're not going to believe this, but this lady wants burglar bars on the upstairs windows to keep her children in!" His supervisor allowed him to do it although it wouldn't pass fire code standards in today's world. It's amazing how we survived during those days without the parameters that we live with today. Suffice it to say, Karen was the only "Hell My Mama Ever Raised" (Johnny Paycheck 1977) and what goes around . . . comes around. I've heard plenty of mothers talk about their most difficult child, and they all state that the child that gave them the most problems will one day have their own "little terror" to raise, and it will be twice the trouble that he or she ever thought about being. Well, on May 28, 1992, Karen met her match in the delivery room with the birth of Andrew Burke Goodwin (Drew), also known as

"Mr. Dynamite." Drew got off to a good start right away by rambunctiously unnerving his mother the way that she so affectionately unraveled Carter and my parents. I'm sure my Mother has sighed, with a pleasant smile, plenty of times, watching Drew pull his antics on Karen the way she always did on others. He's now a teenager, so I'm sure the best he has to give, is yet to come.

After Drew's arrival, we all enjoyed a nice, long, hot summer. Of course, I was still pregnant with Baby Brittain number three, and embracing the summer heat was not near as difficult as I had perceived. My youthful age, at the time may have been the biggest factor in my comfort level as I was still under the age of thirty. Another factor that could have played in my favor was that I was due I early August which meant that I didn't have to endure the entire month of August while pregnant. In fact my due date was actually August 16th, but the doctor was going to do me a favor and deliver the baby two weeks earlier. Obviously, he wasn't delivering the baby early at my request, but at his suggestion to get the baby here before I went into labor. Since I had two previous C- sections, Dr. Schilling wanted to avoid the possibility of labor induced contractions that can cause complications for a scarred uterus. So he scheduled the C-section for August 5, 1992.

The night before the surgery, we took our two girls to Martha' house to be taken care of by her and Mark's sister, Tammy. Tammy is the consummate "Mom in Charge" person, and you could call her the babysitter Nazi. She can run a tight ship, keep everybody in line, and the kids all love her. So we were very comfortable with the kids at Aunt Tammy's Boot Camp. After we dropped them off, we drove back home and prepared the house for the next day's event. It's amazing how nervousness can cause people to do strange things. It's not strange to clean a house, but it is when my husband and I are both cleaning at nine o'clock at night. That nervous energy has to go somewhere, so its best used to get things ready for a big day. We slept well during the night and awakened early the next morning to the blaring sound of the alarm clock reminding us that this was a special day. We readied ourselves for the short drive to the hospital, and away we went.

Once we checked in at the Labor and Delivery department of the hospital, then the nurses took over preparing me for the surgery. Everything went smoothly and it was all very familiar to me since I had been through this routine twice before. I remember the interesting flavor of the antacid drink that they typically give mothers preparing for C-sections. All the protocol was basically the same as it had been in the past, and I behaved well while the anesthesiologist inserted the tube in my lower back for the epidural. I even reminded him of the side effects of the epidural because he was the same anesthesiologist that had given me the same instructions only eighteen months before. After I was all hooked up to the tubes and set for the surgery, Mark and I watched the morning news to catch all the latest information on the day of our daughter's arrival. It was a very pleasant morning, and we just relaxed while we waited for the doctor to arrive. The master of ceremonies, Dr. Schilling, finally arrived in his typical, cheery, mood, and talked to us for a few minutes before going to scrub up. With each step of the morning drill, we were getting closer to obtaining our goal of a healthy delivery for Mom and baby. They finally rolled me into the "holding room" with other patients who were also waiting for surgery. It's a bit barbaric that we were all lined up and waiting for surgery like cattle going to slaughter. I tried to encourage a young boy who was placed next to me as he was having a tonsillectomy. One by one, patients on gurneys, all filed out to meet their respective surgeons and greet the day.

Finally, it was my turn. It was all systems go. Some people seem to think that a C-section is the easy way to deliver a baby. Well, I'm not one of those people. I tend to get a little nervous when it comes to major surgery. During a C-section, the patient is no longer a mother fixating on the natural birth of her child. She's a patient enduring an invasive procedure in order for her baby and herself to survive. There's nothing easy about it! It involves an anesthesiologist, a surgeon, a pediatrician, a staff of neonatal specialist and a host of nurses and assistants to ensure the whole thing goes smoothly. Not only is it a more complicated delivery for everybody involved, but the stress on the body is grueling. First, the patient is strapped down on the operating table which initially causes some anxiety due to the fact that the patient cannot move as they wish. Then a series of medications is administered to the patient causing a variety of responses that engulf the mind and body allowing little or no control from the patient. Once the actual incision is made, the entire abdominal cavity falls prey to successive incisions causing muscles and ligaments to be snipped away in order to reach the uterine wall and remove the baby. While the doctor is performing this procedure, the rest of the body is reacting to the invasive procedure by building up a defense system against this foreign invader. White cell counts can rise in order to build antibodies to fight infection, and blood pressure can fluctuate in response to all the competing factors that the body is undergoing. Finally, the doctor reaches the baby and begins to pull the baby out. When I say pull, I mean just that. Of all the c-sections that I have ever had, I have always felt the doctor literally pull the baby out. It's not uncomfortable; it's just strange to feel the baby literally being removed from your body. After the "tug of war" is over, then I know that soon I'll hear that sweet little sound that makes everybody in the operating room smile.

On this particular day, August 5, 1992, Jordan Belle Brittain, did just that. Much to our relief, Jordan let out a healthy, boisterous cry that let everybody know that she was ready to face the world. She appeared to be as healthy as a Georgia peach! Our pediatrician, Dr. Kauffman, gave Jordan her first check up, while she lay in the incubator, and revealed that she was, indeed, a healthy little, peach. She weighed in at six pounds and ten ounces, and she was twenty inches long. She was the typical weight and size of any normal newborn, but she especially fit the genetic make up of her older sisters. After Jordan received the "all clear" signal from Dr. Kauffman, then the nursing staff continued to clean her up and perform the necessary processes that they do on all newborns. Just before they were ready to take her to the nursery, they let me see her for the first time. My thoughts upon seeing Jordan for the first time concurred with Dr. Kauffman's statement; "She looks just like the rest of them." After our first introduction to each other, the nurses whisked Jordan away to her new place of residence for the next few days. During this time, Dr. Schilling continued to finish up his work on me as he jokingly bragged on himself for performing, once again, another outstanding work of art. Then, I braggingly reminded him of the physically fit, top level gymnast that he was privileged to work on once again! It takes one ham to trump another ham.

During the entire operation, I had tried to pace myself with calm thoughts in order to keep my mind in a healthy perspective while undergoing surgery. It's somewhat awkward lying on an operating table, fully awake, knowing that your body is being cut open. It takes a strong, mental ability to fully comprehend this concept and accept it as something normal. It's not normal. Most surgeries are performed while the patient is asleep under the anesthesia. With C-sections, doctors have found that it is much more beneficial for the mother to be awake during the delivery. First, the mother doesn't have to endure the complexities of anesthesia during and after surgery, and she gets to be awake to see her baby born. Although I agree that these concepts are good, it doesn't make the mental endurance any easier. In other words, it takes a brave person to go through this procedure! With that being said, I had done a good job allowing myself to remain calm during the entire surgery. I could tell that Dr. Schilling was almost finished with me, and I was beginning to breathe a sigh of relief for accomplishing such a masterful feat. At that time, I happened to look up to see the anesthesiologist beginning to put something in my intravenous fluid (IV). I ask him what he was doing, and he said, "I'm giving you something to calm you down; your legs are shaking." I desperately begged him to not give me anything, and I told him that I was just fine. I thought *I'm almost done, and I've made it through; don't do anything to me!* But it was too late. He had his way and administered the sedative. I lost that battle, but I didn't fret over it. I didn't fret over it until the sedative that was supposed to calm me, sent me through the roof! All of a sudden, I wanted to lunge off the operating table and climb the walls! If one can imagine, lying on a gurney, with no feeling in the body from the waist down, tubes and tape strapping the body to the bed, and a feeling in the mind that screams *escape!* I'm literally cut in half from the waist down, and yet, I feel that I need to climb the walls. The panic that engulfed my mind hit catastrophic levels in my brain that radiated throughout my body. To give an analogy of this horrific panic would be to compare the feeling one would have while performing the act of jumping out of an airplane and the parachute doesn't open in time with seconds to go before hitting the earth! How's that for comfort? During this incredible ordeal, I continued to grasp and hold onto the nurse's hand that reached out to me. I remember the nurse well because she had been a nurse at Dr. Schilling's office for a long time. I was surprised to see her in the operating room because I would typically see her only in the office. Her name was Rhonda, and she was my saving grace during that traumatic moment of my life. People, especially nurses, may never know how their tender care for others can have an enormous, endearing affect on their patients and the people around them. Rhonda took exceptional care of me during that time with her gentle manner and loving patience.

Part of what bothered me at the time of this occurrence, was the depth of knowledge that the nursing staff had about my episode. Mental disorders were new to me, so I wasn't aware of how much nurses and doctors at non-psychiatric hospitals knew about treatment for such conditions. I entered the hospital as a maternity patient, not a psychiatric patient. Also, along with this concern was my concern for the probable cause of this ghastly episode, and how long it would last. The whole ordeal probably lasted only a few minutes, but at the time, it felt like hours! In my mind, I thought that I would live in this current state forever. It's normal for most people who experience an unfamiliar episode, of any kind, to feel some anxiety, but when the unfamiliar circumstance is anxiety, then the fear experienced by the person is compounded exponentially.

As Rhonda continued to console me, and the clock ticked away, the anxiety finally, and slowly, began to fade. I was now calm enough to be moved into post-op for recovery without being a disturbance to the other patients. Of course, the recovery room is a scary place all by itself. If I wasn't fearful before, I could easily be terrified in this place. The hospital didn't have a maternity wing for new mothers. Therefore, c-sections were performed in the regular operating room and, patients recovering from c-sections were placed in the same recovery room as all other recovering surgical patients. Basically, the recovery room reminded me of a war zone. People were lying in all kinds of strange positions with lots of tubes and breathing apparatus attached to them. It reminded me of scenes from the hit, television show *MASH*. Not to be unsympathetic, but it didn't provide a very warm and cozy feeling for me. This was not the typical scene that most mothers expect to see after giving birth. New mothers expect a joyful experience at the birth of their child as they have brought new life into the world. It's not exactly the best time to celebrate new life while observing the dastardly effects of surgery on others around you. Anyway, as I lay in my bed, I tried to rest and forget what had just happened. I consistently worked on calming my thoughts and my mind, so that I could regain a sense of well being.

After the allocated amount of time for recovery had past, then it was time for me to be moved on to my own room which, luckily, was on the maternity floor.

As I reached my new room, my head was still spinning somewhat from my previous panic attack. Upon entry to my room, I found that I already had a visitor. Mark, happily, greeted me by saying that I had company, and yet, I was thinking, that I was not ready for company. I thought, *My God man, have you no compassion for what your wife ha just endured?* Apparently, Mark did know what I had been through, as he had been informed by Dr. Schilling. Therefore, he thought it the best medicine for me was to have a guest right off the bat. I was not happy about having a visitor until I realized who it was. It happened to be my dear friend, Susie Grant. So, it was the best medicine after all. Even though I didn't think that I was up for company, it proved a great healing factor for me. As Susie talked, I tried to stay focused on her conversation because it began to pull me out of the drug induced fog that I had been living in for the past several hours. The more I concentrated on Susie, the clearer my mind became. Her visit was heaven-sent after all. With Susie, I never have to worry about anything. I can be at my worst or best with her, and she never seems to be able to tell the difference. That's what true friendship is supposed to be, and I'm thankful for our friendship everyday. That visit began the healing process for me, and got me back on my feet again.

After Susie left, I discovered an interesting fact about my husband. Apparently, during my horrific recovery process he was so concerned about my general health and well being that he called my mother to discuss the name of the baby. In recovery, I had told the nurses that the baby's first name would be Jordan, but that we were undecided about the middle name. I wanted the name Marie. Mark liked the name Belle. I told the nurses that I was certain that he would agree with me; especially after all I had been through. By the time I got to my room on the maternity ward, he and my mother had decided to name the baby's middle name Belle! I said, "No, you and my mother did not do that!" But, oh, indeed, they had! Mark stated, that my mother told him to name that baby what he wanted to name her. So, there you have it. The baby's name is Jordan Belle Brittain, and I was not advised of the decision until after the fact! Of course, I absolutely love the name now, and I wasn't that opposed to it from the beginning. During my pregnancy with Jordan, the movie, Beauty and the Beast, was the biggest box office hit of the day, and naturally, Belle became a popular choice for new baby girls. Mark had never seen the movie, but he just liked the name. I wasn't set on any particular middle name for Jordan at that time, and I wasn't even sure about the name Marie. During the pregnancy, we learned of a woman by the name Jenae Marie, who was a family friend of Mark's family. I liked that name for a baby girl, but we were already set on Jordan for this baby. Nonetheless, we were very happy with the name, but I still couldn't believe that my mother and my husband would conspire against me during my time of need. I must confess I get no respect!

From that point on, I didn't encounter anymore problems with anxiety or panic. Things seemed to go very smoothly for us as we adjusted to our new baby girl. I had decided not to breast feed Jordan because I just wasn't that crazy about it. I had done it enough on the other two babies to realize that it wasn't for me. Of course, I know it's the best thing in the world for the baby, but I wasn't into it. In years past, I've come to realize that women either hate breast feeding, they absolutely love it! There is no grey area about it. As I awakened in the morning of my second day in the hospital, I smiled as I relished in the fact that my breast were neither swelling nor painful. During that time, if a mother did choose to forgo breast feeding, then the doctor prescribed a pill to stop the milk from coming into the breast. So, I awakened with a pleasant start to my day realizing that I had one less obstacle to deal with in my recovery. I was getting close to complete bliss when the pediatrician, Dr. Kauffman, walked in and informed me that Jordan wasn't responding to the formula well, and that I would have to stop taking the pill and start breast feeding! Yes, just like that. I was overruled by a six pound, and ten ounce munchkin! I couldn't believe my luck. With the next feeding, Jordan got her way, and I gave in to her command.

On day three of my hospital stay, I was preparing for release by Dr. Schilling when we found out that Jordan wouldn't be allowed to go home with me. Dr. Kauffman thought that she was still too weak to leave just yet, and I wasn't allowed to stay any longer. Therefore, Mark would have to drive me back and forth to the hospital in order for me to continue to breast feed Jordan. It sounds quite busy going back and forth to the hospital, but conveniently, for us, we lived close to the hospital. Of course, we weren't happy to have to leave Jordan behind, but with the previous experience that we had with Jamie, we knew everything would work out fine. This time we were much calmer about the situation. Mark even joked with Dr. Schilling when he asked if we were leaving without the baby. Mark said, "Yes, don't call us; we'll call you!" On that note, we headed for home to see our other two girls. We tried to look at the bright side of the situation by realizing that we could really take advantage of spending some quality time with Jackie and Jamie before the new baby came home. Once we arrived home, the two girls went crazy with glee upon seeing us for the first time in many days out of the hospital setting. They were all aglow and fluttering us with questions about Jordan and her whereabouts. Jamie, in particular, was curious about the "boo-boo" on my stomach that I had acquired during the delivery. As I sat on the sofa talking with the excited girls, I constantly held a pillow over my belly in case one of them moved too quickly towards my incision. After, we settled in with the girls, and then it was back to getting things in order.

The next day, Mark and I headed back to the hospital to feed Jordan. The hospital staff was very accommodating to us, and gave us a room to enjoy with Jordan. Jordan did great, and she continued to thrive on her new diet. I was adjusting to the feeding process as well, and our new schedule was going great. On one particular visit, as we nestled in our temporary room, we took special notice of a new couple who had just delivered their first baby. Shortly after they checked in to their maternity room, we realized that we knew this couple. They were Rod and Eve Pipkin from McDonough. Eve and I had seen each other several times during our pregnancies at Dr. Schilling's office. She and I would laugh and compare notes on each other's pregnancies, and now, here she was having her baby which was her first. But, the irony wasn't complete yet. Within two days of Mark and me going to the hospital and tending to Jordan, the Pipkins came in, had a baby, and checked out! Some people must know how to do things more efficiently than we do. We're always the first to arrive and the last to leave. The best part is that we all still laugh and talk about it to this day.

Finally, the big day arrived for Jordan to go home. On the day before, when

Rod and Eve left, we remember Eve dressing up her baby for her first debut. When we left with Jordan, she went home in her hospital gown! We were doing good just to all be going home together. Once we arrived home, Jackie and Jamie were all "keyed up" over Jordan. They were so excited to see their little sister at home, and we all enjoyed a great reunion together with the girls. Now that Jordan was home, we took an inventory of the girl's ages; Jackie was three years old, Jamie was seventeen months, and Jordan was one week old. Mark and I knew then that we were out numbered by a group of very young munchkins, but we had no idea how challenging our new role as parents could be.

Chapter Three

Living in Darkness

Mark and I had come to realize that postpartum time could mean trouble time for me. With the previous knowledge that we had about my mental condition, we knew to monitor my health closely. We also had comfort in knowing a good doctor that we could trust along with a medication that we knew could work. So, the game plan was that if I started to experience any problems, then we would go see Dr. RB and start back on the medication. With that, we felt comfortable moving into the future. I wish I could say that it was that simple, but it wasn't.

Our trouble first began with the sale of our house which occurred just three weeks before Jordan was born. I didn't want to move and I was dreading the thought of moving anywhere. The house that we lived in was my favorite house of all time. I was very content living in our home and living in the town of McDonough, Georgia. We had established friends in our neighborhood and around town that we enjoyed very much. Life was perfect for us and we all thrived in that environment. But, Mark had bigger dreams for us that I had not anticipated. He's always the big thinker, reaching way out of "the box" to strive for his goals for our family. I, on the other hand, am happy with a roof over my head and food to eat. Even though we had different dreams, I understood that Mark always knew best.

With the house sold, we had only three weeks to pack up and move. Of course, I couldn't do any packing or lifting since I was still recovering from surgery. So Mark, along with some friends, had the full time job of packing and moving everything. We were moving into temporary housing in a rental house in Decatur, Georgia where Mark's mother, Martha, lived. She had bought the house as an investment just before we had Jordan. She offered it to us, free of rent, to live in while we built our new house in McDonough. It was an offer that we couldn't refuse, so we took it. However good the offer, I did try to refuse it by researching rental houses McDonough and the surrounding areas. Even though most people would be ecstatic over the deal from Mark's mother, I although appreciative, was desperate to stay close to home. I searched and researched everything in our area the weeks before I had Jordan, but nothing materialized. I was at a loss. I could handle living in temporary quarters, building a new house and raising the three small children easily if I could just stay in my newly adopted home town of McDonough, Georgia. But that was not to be. My problems with moving to this house in Decatur were many. First, the neighborhood that we would be living in was not conducive to young families with small children. Most of our neighbors would be at retirement age and above which didn't leave a lot of room for commonality between us. Secondly, the houses were built in the 1960's, which meant that they had low ceilings, dark wood and outdated furnishings. I certainly don't seemed to come across as a stuffy, spoiled brat, but I had become accustomed to newer house plans that had tall ceilings, brightly colored walls and lots of sunlight coming through to almost every room in the house. The two houses that Mark and I had started off in were modest starter homes. I certainly didn't need the Taj Ma Hal; I just needed positive energy. There were a few other issues with this house that made me nervous. The reason that the house had come up for sale was because the previous owner had died by committing suicide in the garage! How's that's for positive energy? That's just the type of environment that I want to bring my newborn baby into right from the start. The Chinese, proverbial Gods would have a conniption fit over a house with this type of karma, but it was all we had. So, on September 3, 1992 were packed up and headed out. And that's where my sadness began.

In the midst of the day on September third, we received a phone call that a dear friend of ours, Howard, who was dying from cancer, probably wouldn't make it through the day. Mark desperately wanted to go see Howard that day before it was too late, but he couldn't leave his family in the middle of a move. Howard had been a good friend of Mark's mother for many years and had helped the family out a lot since Mark's Dad had died in 1970. He was absolutely a brilliant man, and he would give you the shirt off of his back. He was diagnosed with lymphoma a year earlier, and now he was losing the battle. The minute that we drove into the driveway of the Decatur home, someone announced that Howard was gone. Upon hearing the news, we bowed our heads in grief for a moment, and then proceeded with the project of unpacking and setting up house. There was a somber, reluctant mood in our actions as we continued to work on the house while reflecting back on happier times spent with Howard. Time was not on our side in the respect of grieving the loss of a loved one while withstanding the unpredictable process of a major move. Feeling a sense of loss and overwhelmed with responsibilities made our efforts much more arduous, but we continued on as we had little or no options.

The first night that we slept in our new dwelling, we were quickly awakened by baby Jordan who apparently had caught a cold somewhere along the way. Mark got up along with me to assist with the baby. While we were in the kitchen getting the baby some medicine and a fresh bottle of water, we noticed an incredible amount of some type of grainy substance on the linoleum floor. Mark commented that it had been scrubbed many times, but it still wasn't clean enough. We were already talking about how nice our previous home was and how much we already missed it. The reality of this new and somewhat depressing situation was beginning to register with us and bring us down. After our initial discussion in the kitchen, I looked around to find Jordan's pacifier and spotted it up on the mantle over the fireplace. As I reached for it, I spotted something sitting on it. I screamed as I realized what it was a slug sucking on the baby's pacifier! Needless to say, the odds were against us and our world seemed to be sinking into total disillusion. With such a warm welcome to the new house, it's no wonder that things went down hill from the start. We begrudgingly continued to settle into this house of horrors and make the best of our, hopefully, short stay in this dwelling. Every morning Mark would get up and get ready for work, and then he would drive forty minutes away to the office. I would get up with him and prepare Jackie and Jamie for the pre-school that they attended at a local church. We plotted along in this routine course of daily activities just trying to bring up another tomorrow. Every part of our lives was typical for young families at this stage in the game. However, as the days past, I started to succumb to the chemical imbalances that were beginning to take place in my brain. Combining postpartum blues, the environmental conditions under which we were living, the loss of a friend through death, and raising three small children, it was inevitable that nature would have its way and that my condition would get worse before it got better. And that's exactly what happened over the next nine months. Most people relate a nine month period to someone having a baby. For me, it took as long for me to recover from having a baby as it did for me to carry through the pregnancy.

There were times when the depression would hit me hard and then, without notice, the fog would lift. On one such occurrence, I was sitting at the pre-school with Jackie and her class, and I remember thinking that I was fine in that particular setting where I was away from the house. I continued to think of ways that we could move back to McDonough where I could return to a normal and happy existence. After I left Jackie's class and drove back home, I would succumb to the murky shadows of gloom that began to engulf me as I approached the house. After a while, I became more convinced that moving back to McDonough was the only thing that would help me. I begged Mark to take us back home, but he rationally insisted that we would not do anything so absurd. Once the waves of depression had begun, I continued in my battle to conquer the condition and improve my mental attitude about the house. I was doing my best to search and to continue searching for the answers to this sinister predicament that I was living in everyday. I was looking for help at every avenue, except for calling Dr. RB because, once again, I felt that I needed to be a stronger person who was capable of handling life's tough problems. After a month of trying that method, I finally relented and called Dr. RB for some help. He prescribed the same antidepressant that I had taken after I had Jamie which was thought to be the magic cure for me. Dr. RB, Mark and I all thought that this medicine would take care of my symptoms, and that I would respond well as I had before. However, after a couple of months, we all noticed that I wasn't responding nearly as well to the medicine as I had before. At that point, Dr. RB began to try different antidepressants on me such as Prozac, Zoloft and many others, but none of them worked. By this time we were into the holidays with a lot going on. Even though we were busy, it wasn't enough to distract me out of my illness. Basically, I pushed myself to go with the flow of hectic events and holiday gatherings. While attending my family's Christmas party, I tried desperately to put a smile on my face and pretend that I was fine, so that nobody would notice my symptoms. No matter how sick I may be, I still stand by my motto, "never let them see you sweat!"

After the holidays, Mark and I regrouped with Dr. RB to discuss other options of treatment that were available. The remaining treatment options appeared less than favorable for the two of us as we listened while Dr. RB discussed the severity of taking such serious medications. Apparently, we had stepped into a deeper hole with this illness allowing greater complications and more intense treatment. The next level of medications would require regular blood tests to monitor the enzyme levels of my liver as well as other factors in order to insure my physical health while undergoing this treatment. Dr. RB explained to us his first choice of medication for me would be lithium. After we discussed the benefits and burdens of this medicine, then Mark and I left his office and decided that we would think about it. Mark was more nervous than I was about this new option of medicine, and he wasn't the least bit happy about it. His theory was that we had tried medicines that didn't work, and now the doctor was prescribing a more, intense medicine with possible grave, side effects and no guarantee of wellness. Shortly after this particular office visit and after much discussion with Mark, I decided that I just needed to toughen up, get over my negative mental attitude, and maybe seek the help of a Christian Counselor. I thought that I should be stronger than all of this, and that it was almost shameful for me to be so out of control. In my mind, I thought that I should be able to conquer this situation without the help of medicine. I was still viewing my situation with the frame of mind that this was not a medical condition, but that it was a situation that I should have control over. From this point, we declined the medicine route, and I decided to seek Christian Counseling.

Christian Counseling proved to be quite interesting and not the least bit helpful! For two months I poured out all my pent up sadness and frustration, not to mention a host of already confessed sins, to a woman that I hardly knew, and who never started a session without receiving a payment from me first! To this day, I don't remember any advice that she gave me. After this futile attempt, I was ready to start back with Dr. RB. Once back in the doctor's care, Mark and I carefully listened to his instructions and followed his advice. Dr. RB explained that if the lithium did work, then we would see results within six weeks. It's very strange to go to the doctor for a cure, yet, the cure comes in the form of trial and error. I, like most people, am use to going to the doctor and getting a quick fix for any typical problem that may arise. However, I've had to learn the hard way, that mental illness is a delicate condition with no exact cure. It's not like getting an antibiotic to treat specific bacteria that can be positively identified by a culture test. There is no exact science to treating mental illnesses, although researchers are getting closer everyday to matching up specific medicines with specific symptoms and receiving beneficial results more quickly. The medical science behind mental disorders has come a long way since I was first diagnosed with my condition. Once we received our instruction from Dr. RB, Mark and I moved on with some hope for improvement in my symptoms in the near future. And from that point, my story took an interesting twist.

As I began my medicine, we were still living in the house from hell where the fragrance in the air smelled of doom, but I still alive and adjusting accordingly. However, now we were closer than ever to making the big move back to the big city of McDonough, Georgia! Despite the fact that I was slowly sinking into a dark abyss, was content that the time had finally come for us to move back to our beloved, adopted town of McDonough. I spent all my days aggressively packing and loading everything in the house, so that the move would be smooth and easy. I really didn't care how smooth things went, I was just happy to be packing to go back home! I finally had a fulfilling purpose again and something exciting to look forward to in the days ahead. All of our friends were living in McDonough, and I couldn't wait to see them again. I also, was anxious to get back into my familiar routine in our home town with all my favorite stores and places to visit. Needless to say, I was regaining some of the joy that had escaped me for the last six months.

Finally, the greatest day of our lives had arrived! It was moving day, and I was ecstatic! The more vacant the rental house became during the loading of the moving truck, the better off I became. It was like graduating from College, or the aftermath of conquering some magnificent feat, where I felt a great sense of accomplishment in making it through such difficult times. I had passed the test, and I was being rewarded for my effort! Now, I could have my life back. Once we were in the car heading back home, I couldn't believe that our ordeal was over, and that we were really headed back home. I was like a kid out of school. When we reached the newly built house, the kids swarmed the dwelling with such excitement that they could hardly contain themselves. They ran and checked out every room, quickly claiming which one would be their bedroom for life. Of course, little Jordan didn't have much of a choice since she was only six months old. Even though it was a busy day of unloading, we were joyfully going about our business of unpacking and setting up house. I remained enthusiastic about finally being at home again, especially in such a bright and beautiful, new house! Even though I was happy to be back, mentally I was still suffering to some degree. Of course, Mark and I knew that I wasn't cured, yet from my depression and anxiety, but we felt confident that the medicine, given some time, would kick in and work. Everything seemed to be going in the right direction, and soon we could get our lives back completely.

Over the next few days, we continued to unpack and put things away, and friends dropped in to welcome us back to town. It was a joyous time and, yet, I was continuing to fight an undercurrent of anxiety that could suddenly swell up in me without notice. I remember one time, in particular, when a friend and neighbor, Kathy Bush, stopped by in the morning to see the girls and me and to see how things were going. I remember talking to her, as we were standing by my butler's pantry and my anxiety level sky-rocketed so high that I thought I wouldn't be able to contain the explosion going off in my head. I intensely held my composure, and I didn't think that Kathy ever noticed. Episodes, like this one, kept occurring, and I had very little control over them. A few days later, Mark was ready to go out and celebrate our homecoming at Eagle's Landing Country Club. We had friends joining us there for dinner. I sat through most of the cocktail hour, and obviously I was not drinking any alcohol due to my situation. Shortly before dinner arrived, I began feeling more and more anxiety stirring in my head. As people approached me throughout the evening, I felt as if I was being torpedoed by over-information. Each face that came towards me was a bullet of information that my brain couldn't process. It was like having tunnel vision where you are in your own world, and everything going on around you is outside of your world. That's the kind of experience that I was having, only the outer world was attacking me as each face approached me, and I couldn't handle the overload of data. The ability of my brain to receive information was at a minimum, and I was shutting down. I told Mark that we needed to leave and go home which didn't please him at all. He wasn't being unsympathetic; he just hadn't grasped the idea that I was entering a new stage of the disorder that neither of us had experienced yet. We finally did excuse ourselves from our company, and headed back home, with both of us disappointed at my condition. When I awoke the next morning, I began the day with the usual flare of sending kids off to school and cleaning house. Then, suddenly, before I knew what was happening, my mind and body began to swirl with an intoxication of energy that could not be controlled. We'd all like to have more energy at times, but no one wants it at this level. My symptoms began with restlessness. I couldn't sit down and be comfortable. I couldn't sit and watch TV in order to get myself focused on something else. I could not do anything but move constantly! Five minutes felt like five years. I was literally becoming a prisoner in my mind and body. It's unbearable to live in a constant state of continuous anxiety where the chemicals in your brain dictate a perpetual condition with no end in sight. It's incredibly alarming living in this condition for one second much less living in it for hours on end with no hope of recovery. At this point, I called Mark and told him what was going on with me. He immediately called Dr. RB and got the wheels in motion. This was the first day, of the rest of my life, living in my own private hell for the next several months.

Later that day, Mark brought home the medicine that Dr. RB had prescribed for me. Mark and I had both talked to Dr. RB on the phone earlier in the day, and I described my symptoms to him. He correlated my situation to that of a "train out of control," and told me that we needed to put on the brakes quickly! Thus, the new medicine that he prescribed for me was trilafon; a medicine that would calm me down and slow down the processes of the brain. Once again, most people would welcome a tranquilizer to help their mood during the day. That wasn't the case with this medicine and my mood. Everything was already out of control, so nothing felt good. The new medicine turned me from my restless state into a zombie. I was calm and relieved that the restlessness was gone, but the alternative wasn't much better. At this point, I began my descent into the pit of depression which I stayed in for the next several months. Now I was living without feelings or emotions. My life was an empty vessel. My body and my mind were trapped in the devil's pen with no hope for escape. Depression renders its victims void of any and all emotion. When people experience heartache and emotional turmoil over circumstances that life dishes out, that seem unfair, such as a broken relationship or a death of a loved one, we endure tremendous heartache. Sometimes we wish we didn't have emotions in order to avoid feeling the pain from some horrific event in our lives. I'm here to tell everyone that emotional pain is considered heavenly bliss to one suffering from depression. If you can feel and experience emotions for any reason, I don't care how sad or traumatic, it is far better than the alternatives, which are death, itself, or depression. As I was living day in and day out with my depression, I thought of many other conditions that I would welcome, if I had a choice, over depression. I know that I haven't walked in the shoes of a cancer patient going through treatment, and I know that cancer has it's many demons, but, at least cancer doesn't take away a person's right to feel the love of others who care for them.  Prisoners, sitting on death row, still have the ability to feel their emotions about their impending doom, and can still have the desire to live.  Not only do they have those options, but they can still reach out to a God who hasn't forsaken them, and ask for forgiveness.  For those of us living with depression, our rights and privileges dealing with emotion is taken away from us. People with neuromuscular diseases such as Lou Gehrig's disease, multiple sclerosis, muscular dystrophy and such, endure tremendous suffering, but as long as they can feel the love of others and have the desire to live, then they are more fortunate than a person with depression.  These comparisons may sound desperate and far-reaching, but they convey the endless agony of a person living with depression.  When a person falls prey to depression, they never know the longevity of the disease.  We don't have the benefit of knowing that this condition will last ten days while taking an antibiotic as we most assuredly know with common illnesses that can affect our daily lives.  When we go to the doctor for answers and cures, they doctor's only words are, "We don't know the cure; we just have to try different medicines until we get a response."  Getting a response is also not an absolute.  We have no guarantees of ever recovering.  The last resort is shock therapy, which I have read about in a fantastic book that further describes depression, titled *Undercurrents*, by Martha Manning.  A highly recommend this book for reading about depression.

So, as I began my life in this depressive state, I tried my best to deal with it.

For the first four days on this new treatment, I was to take the medicine, trilafon, four times a day. Obviously, that dosage kept me pretty sedated. I basically went through the motions of life without ever feeling a part of anything. The first weekend of this new journey, Mark brought home Chick-fil-a sandwiches for everyone for lunch. He set us all up at the kitchen table to eat together. I remember walking to the table, trying to act as normal as possible, and attempting to eat. I got down a whole half of a sandwich, and that was it. Food had absolutely no taste and gave no satisfaction. It helped, only minutely, to squelch a minor amount of hunger that sometimes came to surface. And that was about the entire fulfillment that food had to offer me. After lunch, I returned back to the den to recline on the sofa and attempt to watch some TV for what little entertainment that it could provide. And, thus, this began my new routine of my mundane life. After the first four days, Dr. RB cut back on the dosage of taking four pills a day, to taking three pills a day. He was gradually pulling back on the severe sedation that was so necessary in the beginning. He also, started me on a new medicine to treat my overall condition, like the lithium was supposed to do. It was called tegretol. He kept me on the Lithium also, because he thought the combination might work well together. Like I've stated before, there is no exact science in the world of mental illness. So here we go with just what my husband was afraid of occurring; more medicine. At this point, I didn't care. Anything was better than the state in which I was living. And, thus, I started on a new medicine that caused more concern for Mark and a vague amount of hope for either of us as to the cure. Since we were in such a plight of exploration for a remedy, my sister, Karen, thought that taking me to an herbalist who used natural, herbal medicines and massage therapy might help. We tried it, but Dr. RB was definitely against any herbal medicines, what so ever, and the massage left me still looking for answers. However, I do remember experiencing, for the first time, the warmth of the therapist's hand as she placed it on the middle of my back. I could not believe the amount of heat that radiated from her hand into my back. I thought she must be some kind of psychic to have those powers! Anyway, Karen drove me back home, and I continued on the treatment program originally set up by Dr. RB.

All we could do now was to live life as normally as possible and hope and pray for healing. Needless to say, Mark became "Mr. Mom" for quite a while. He hired a nanny to take care of the children and me during the day, and he took over at night. The nanny's name was Vicki, and she was very young. She proved to be very good at her job, and she seemed to not be bothered by my "weirdness". I never worried about acting strange in front of her, because she seemed unaffected by my behavior. She related to the girls well, so she worked out well for us. Basically, my days would begin with me crying to Mark and telling him that I felt terrible, and that I couldn't go on living this way for long. I quickly learned that crying to him only made things worse for him, and it wouldn't bring a cure for me. I was like a child who cries out to its mother to fix a skin wound or bandage a cut, and ultimately make everything well again. Only this time, no one could help me. I was living in this private void, life where no one could reach me. I was living in my own abyss, endlessly tormented with emptiness. Every step that I took to perform routine tasks for the day was ladled with a thick grey cloud of suppression. My footsteps were weighted as I *lunged* forward to move my limbs in order to complete even the simplest of tasks. Every action that I took was haunted with numbness. Every breath I took felt like a useless vapor. I moved about the house pushing onward to keep some functionality about myself and my purpose for existing. I put forth considerable effort to run the house while living under house arrest. House arrest was just how my life was. Everything inside me had been arrested and belonged to something else that no one understood. I moved through the day slowly drifting from room to room to clean and keep busy. Chores needed to be done, and that was my job as a mother and homemaker. Even though I had assistance from Vickie, she had her errands to do, and I had mine. My goal was to do as much of the work load as possible in hopes that I could stimulate my mind out of the stagnate state that I was in. Nonetheless, accomplishing any of the chores was indeed a chore in itself. Once again, every move I made felt weighted down by an invisible tonnage of mass surrounding my body. Simply lifting clothes in and out of the washer and dryer took considerable effort. It took so much effort, that it was easy to just give up, not mentioning that there was never any real desire, on my part, for the clothes to be washed. I was simply going through the motions. Even when the kids came home from school, they didn't matter to me. It didn't matter to me if they existed or not because I didn't feel my own existence. The world had absolutely no meaning for me at all. Depression robs it's victims of life. It takes away all reasons for living. Healthy people don't understand that life can lose its purpose, and they believe that there is always a reason to live. And that's the key to life . . . a reason to live. When you have depression, reason does not exist. Reason is dead just like the depressed person is dead on the inside. Everything that ever made me the person that I was . . . had died. That's why suicide doesn't look too frightening to a person with depression. Living under this spell of evil, makes death look inviting. Depressed people don't want to die; they just want to feel well again, and if medicine can't help them, then death appears as the only cure. It's the equivalent of a person living with tremendous pain and being expected to live the rest of his or her life in that condition with little or no hope for a cure. And the depressed patient does live with excruciating pain; only it comes in the form of numbness. Under these circumstances, life parallels the vegetative state of victims lying unconscious and comatose with varying degrees of brain activity that can be recorded on a monitor. The only difference between a comatose patient and a depressed victim is that the person living in the vegetative state isn't acutely aware of his or her present condition, and the depressed person can't get away from the constant anguish of living day in and day out in a hollow shell.

Apparently, and unbeknownst to me, I had exuded some signs that I might be contemplating suicide. I don't remember ever expressing my thoughts about suicide to anyone. However, I must have given away some clues because my sister, Diane, talked to me about it one day. One particular day, Diane broached the subject with me, and I was quite surprised and shocked because I didn't think that I dwelled on that gruesome topic too much. Since Diane was not an overly religious person, I was definitely taken aback by what she said. She brought up the matter to me, and then, she basically said that it was not my choice to make. From her words, I detected a sense of fear as she tried to portray God's reluctance to forgive such a sin. Whether it's true or not, it was enough to scare me away from any further thoughts on the issue. Once again, this message, coming from Diane, who believes in God, but doesn't express her feelings about him very often, made her statement even more credible. When healthy, I, like most people, shied away from the subject matter of suicide due to the fact that it's a puzzling and frightening entity. We live in a world with different religions and different opinions on this and other matters, yet we have one God and his book, the Bible, that clearly defines the answers to all of life's most mysterious questions.

As desperate as I was, living under this veil of gloom, at least I had the ability to understand the meaning of the word scared. Since I realized that suicide would mean the end of my earthly life, but more importantly, to me, it could possibly mean the absence of my eternal life that I had been counting on since the age of eight when I accepted Jesus Christ as my Lord and Savior, then I decided that nothing was worth the risk of losing my salvation. Now I was becoming fixated on a new and inspirational word, scared, could it be possible that my brain was beginning to correct the errors of its ways? Did God still know me? Did he know where I was and where I had been? Why? Why this? Why me? However, the question, "Why me?" was quickly followed, in thought, with, *I'd rather it be me that had been dealt this fate than anyone else in the world.* I would never wish this dastardly illness on anyone! I am convinced that the worst hell a person, living on this earth, can suffer is depression and other disorders of the mind. It was at this point that I began to realize that despite the delirium of my mind, that I still processed one, very important function . . . the consciousness of my faith. In the midst of all the darkness, I could still find God. However faint my recollection of him was, I could still remember the times of my life when I needed him most, and how he had always been there. I remembered all the promises the Bible had revealed to me through the years about God and his miraculous acts of healing people and raising Lazarus from the dead. I recalled preachers, preaching from the pulpit, telling endearing stories of his love and of his abilities to always lift us up. Most of all, I knew that he would never leave me. It was with this realization that I began to believe, with only an ounce of hope, that one day this, too, would pass.

From that revelation, I continued to live day in and day out with the grueling disease that marred my life and profusely poisoned my mind. However feeble and dysfunctional I was, Mark was determined to still take me out in public from time to time on an "as needed" basis to attend social events that he felt were important for us. I was horrifically embarrassed for anyone to see me as I appeared then, but, according to Mark, I didn't have a choice. One of our first encounters out was some, swanky function that involved the law firm, and I was hoping against hope that no one would notice anything different about me. Even though I knew that everyone was aware of my condition, no one had seen me out in public living in this condition and under the influence of so many medicines! Believe me, they did notice, and they did ask questions. Mark's senior partner, Buddy Welch, showed the most concern. However embarrassing it was for me, I was amazed at how wonderfully well everyone responded to me. I had never been one to show my shortcomings in front of anyone, much less in a social setting. I was pleasantly surprised at the outpouring of support that I received from all the attendees that night.

On another occasion, Mark invited some of our back door neighbors over for a glass of wine. Once again, I performed to the best of my abilities, trying to hide any flaws that I had, and once again, these people took notice. After that gathering, our guest, Floyd Pennington and his wife, Diana, inquired to Mark about my state of well being. I have since laughed at Floyd's reaction as he said to Mark, "Man you got to get her off that stuff (meaning the medicine). He continued, "She's drugged up!" Mark explained to the best of his ability the situation to Floyd and Diana, but they were not easily convinced. Also, a few days later, some very dear people, and friends of mine, decided to take me out to lunch at the Country Club and enjoy the LPGA which was hosted by Eagle's Landing Country Club annually. Trish Brunner and Jean Hanger graciously took me under their angelic wings in effort to nourish me back to health. Trish, a registered nurse and Jean, a fun-loving socialite, took the time to get me out of the house and to mentor me back to reality. Their hearts' desires to reach out and help me during this most difficult time of my life will be forever engraved in my heart with loving thankfulness.

After attempting these latest outings, I decided that I could do more on a daily basis, and so I started venturing out with Vikki, the nanny, to run errands locally. I'll never forget going to my favorite Hallmark store, called Gloria's Hallmark, which was located a good distance from town square in McDonough. Gloria was a long time McDonough resident, and her husband, Tony Moye, was also a native of the quaint, little town and a local pharmacist who owned Moye's Pharmacy. During this particular time of the illness, my walking ability was greatly skewed with a debilitating shuffle of my feet and a hunched back that highly resembled Parkinson's disease. I now laugh, as I almost did then, at Gloria's reaction as she came over to see me in my "funky" condition. She asked, "What's going on here?" I loved her blatant honesty about my new look! When someone feels comfortable enough to speak the truth to you, no matter the situation, then it sends you an instant message that you are accepted for who you are. That's why I chuckled so easily at Gloria's response. She made me feel relaxed right away. I'd like to acknowledge Gloria for her genuine expression of friendship. People need to know that it the small acts of a kindness that leave a lasting impression on others and that's one of the most important things in life. I regret to mention, since that time, we have lost Gloria to breast cancer. Many years after this occurrence, she was diagnosed with cancer, and unfortunately, she died just a few weeks later. By the time everyone was learning of the news, it was too late to say good bye. Gloria was a special and kind person to everyone she met, and she is sorely missed today.

Now that I was initiating my own out-of-the-house excursions, it was a good sign that possibly my mental health was improving. However the glimmer of hope that it was, I was still very much living in my own little cave of darkness. At my next check up with Dr. RB, Mark and I mentioned the Parkinson's appearance that I exuded and asked if something could be done about it. We had both become so accustom to the negative side of my condition, that we just assumed it was a part of my illness that we would just have to endure it. And, then, out of the blue, Dr. RB said, "Oh, we have a pill for that!" Some people may think that all Dr. RB does is pump drugs into my system, which is what Mark had originally feared, but now, we were use to the idea. It brought great comfort knowing that something could be done to correct the problem. In fact, Mark wanted to ask Dr. RB why he hadn't already suggested the idea start me on the medicine. But now that was a moot point. We didn't care anymore, we were just ready to move forward, and do what needed to be done in order to get me well. After the first dose that I took of the new medicine, artane, my posture erected itself back to complete normalcy. Dr. RB explained that the posture that I had previously carried before I started on the artane was indeed the exact same posture as that of a Parkinson's patient. So, when I say that I walked around like a little old lady, I meant it.

Mark and I were so relieved that my posture was back, and that I could now look somewhat normal out in public. Now, let's sum up all the medicines that I was taking; lithium, tegretol and artane. It's a good thing that I never tried any "recreational" drugs during my youthful years, because adjusting to all of these prescription medications was a trip all on its own! Now that I had two months under my belt of taking the lithium and the tegretol, something stirred within me, and I felt a change. I'll never forget the sun-filled day when my next door neighbor, Kathy Hubert, walked over to my house and said to me, and said, "Your eyes look better." I was significantly enlightened at her sincere observation! I told her, that I had just begun to feel an inkling of light seep into my mind for the very first time in nine lonely and long months. This sparkle of light was so slight and demure, but, yet it radiated an enormous amount of hope for someone living in darkness for so long. This slight increase in improvement felt incredibly huge compared to the burdensome load that I had carried around for so long. It was simply amazing the difference I felt with only a minor change. Apparently, the tegretol had kicked in and had begun to work, and miraculously, I was responding to it beautifully. Mark conceded the same as Kathy had about the subtle change in my overall countenance when he came home from work that very same evening. We all had reason to be hopeful for a new day and a new beginning for me as well as everyone involved, who had endured the trials and tribulations of this atrocious quandary with me. Dr. RB was also relieved with the good news and positive signs of my improving progress, but he was also cautious to not change anything involving the medicines. He decided to keep me on the Lithium along with the tegretol because he wasn't sure if it was the tegretol alone that was helping me or the combination of the two medicines working together. Mark and I thought that

Dr. RB's advice made good sense, and we were happy to oblige. From that glorious day when Kathy Hubert and Mark noticed the small, twinkle of hope radiate in my eyes, I continued to improve. That was the first day of my life coming out of the darkness and back into the light. It was a fragile and delicate process, but the pieces were coming together for the first time in nine months.

Chapter Four

The Journey Back

    Hip, hip horary, I was back among the living and fully operating the house and completely capable of driving the children to all their prospective places. The mounting signs of improvements made it clear that I was officially re-entering the game of life. By the end of May, 1993, I was continuing to notice even greater improvements in my disposition. One night, Mark and I were preparing to go out to a major party, a fundraiser for the local hospital, Henry Medical Center. I was busy getting ready for one of my first big outings in a long time. As I was getting ready for the party, I couldn't help but notice that I was going about business like nothing ever happened. I couldn't believe how ready I was to go out and socialize again. It was almost as if I had been healed overnight. Once at the party, I conversed with people with no problem at all. Mark and I danced, and mingled around with the crowd as we had always done before. I couldn't believe how well I was doing! We had a delightful time, and it was definitely the beginning of our new lives living out from under the cloud of depression. I still had a ways to go in my recovery, but I was feeling great to be able to enjoy life again. I was finally content within my mind and body again. I could sleep well at night and take care of my family during the day. We still kept the nanny with us because I still needed help around the house with three kids, and although I was doing much better, I needed more time to overcome certain challenging obstacles. I could do most things around the house, and I could assist Vicki with a lot of the household chores that she had been totally responsible before. I felt great! It felt so good to feel good again! I was overcome with joy. My days were simple, and that was just fine with me. Knowing that I could take care of my family during the day, and that I could look forward to a relaxing night, was all I needed in life. I didn't ever expect to get any better than I was at this time. Some of the obstacles that I still face were grocery shopping and driving long distances. I needed assistance in grocery stores because the warehouse sized buildings where quite overwhelming for me, and I could easily get panicky in such a vast space. Wide, open spaces and long narrow aisles were bothersome for me. The panic feeling could come over me at anytime in those places. The panic that I would feel was paralyzing for me and quite uncomfortable. It was also embarrassing to think that others in the store could see me if I experienced such an attack. Vanity is still everything for a girl raised in the south with the manners of Emily Post. There were other limitations that I had during this time. Being the active, athlete that I had always been, I longed to get back into the routine of exercise. And, of course, exercise is a terrific healer for every illness. But, it's difficult to exercise when you can't take a walk around the block without having a panic attack. I experienced many panic attacks during my nine months living in bondage. During that dreadful time, I couldn't even make it fifty feet down to the mail box without having an attack. Now I could make it past the mailbox, but not much further by myself. That's where another angel came in to help me out. A neighbor, Barbra Kelley, had heard of my predicament, and she offered to come over to my house and take me on walks. So during the summer of 1993, Barbra and I would walk a couple of miles every morning. We had such a wonderful time talking and walking on those breezy summer mornings. She also made me feel so comfortable, and she was so accepting of me in my vulnerable situation. That's just something that I wasn't use to people doing. I wasn't use to people accepting other people's flaws. Although this was a new concept for me, I was able to accept Barbra's kindness without worry of rejection. There had been other times during my nine months of confinement to the house, where I tried to do aerobic videos at home to get exercise. But it was a futile effort since my coordination was completely off. It was such a strange feeling to have previously had great abilities in the arena of athletics as a cheerleader and a gymnast all my life, and now I couldn't put one foot in front of the other without stumbling. One particular exercise video tape that I tried to do, required me to move my left arm to the left and my right arm to the right in a rhythmical pattern. No matter how hard I tried to get my mind and body together in a coordinated pattern, I simply couldn't do it. For a former athlete, this revelation was devastating. But now, Barbra had me back on track. When I wasn't walking with her, I did attempt to do some exercise tapes at home, and I was more successful.

While I was getting things back together on the home front, Dr. RB was also busy trying to fine tune my medicines in order to give me more flexibility and freedom with my life. His goal was always to get me back to a normal, functioning status that was appropriate for me and eventually remove the medicines one at a time until I could live without them. So, he tried many different anti-depressants that could improve my mood even more than it was and provide relief from the anxiety that still plagued me. This process took two years to complete. There would be times when a new medicine would work great, but I would experience nausea with it. I would take the anti-nausea medicine, phenergan, to counteract the nausea, and go about my merry way. And I'm not talking about taking the oral form of phenergan. I took the old fashioned remedy that your mother would give you in the buttocks. It didn't bother me at all to conform to this type of lifestyle since the concoction seemed to work. I had learned the hard way that relief is the key to success no matter how you administer the medicine. Women can handle anything; especially when we get favorable results from the cure at hand. We are not a proud bunch when it comes to medicines that can have proven themselves worthy no matter the amount of picking and probing that we undergo. I was content to stay with this current method of treatment because I was so desperate to find the solution to my chronic anxiety. Dr. RB said that I could not stay on this medicine and continue to use phenergan everyday because the phenergan would eventually create terrible side effects. I shuttered to ask what those side effects could possibly be. Ignorance is bliss, so I dropped any questioning ideas that popped into my head. All I needed to know was that if Dr. RB said no, then it was a definite, no. So he continued to recommend new medicines for me to try, and I continued to discover different side effects to each one that had never been known before. After two years of research and repeated trials on different medicines, Dr. RB found a new drug, called klonopin that was designed to specifically treat anxiety and panic attacks. Thus, my venture into this new drug therapy appeared promising and interesting.

After two weeks on this drug, I began to notice a side effect where I felt like I was having head rushes. That was the only way I could describe the sensation. I didn't think anything about it since I was use to experiencing different side effects from different medicines. I assumed that it would soon pass with time as was the case with the other unusual symptoms that I had encountered in the past from attempts with different medications. Sometimes the occurrences with the head rush were also accompanied by a feeling of light headedness. When the head rush made me feel too lightheaded, then I would lie down for about fifteen minutes, and then it would go away. Other than that, I continued on with my regular house work and errand running. I had even started back exercising, and I was jogging in the neighborhood by myself. At my next appointment with Dr. RB, I mentioned the head rush symptoms that I was having. He took my pulse, and said "Your pulse is skipping a beat." Then he suggested that I see a cardiologist soon. The next day, I called a doctor friend of ours, Jim Barlow, to ask for a referral on a good cardiologist. He suggested Dr. Howard Snapper. I proceeded to set up an appointment with Dr. Snapper whose office was located in Riverdale, Georgia. I was surprised at the quick availability for an appointment with him. Mark took me to the appointment and sat with me curious as to what the outcome of this visit could mean. Okay, this story gets funny and scary at the same time. The nurse hooked me up to the electrocardiogram (EKG). She came back into the room a few minutes later to repeat the test because she said that the machine had messed up. After repeated tries, she finally handed the results to Dr. Snapper. Mark had left the room when my test was being done, and as he came back into the room, he noticed five doctors analyzing my results. He said, "Well dear, you've baffled them again." He and I just laughed about it. When Dr. Snapper came back into my room, he informed Mark and me, that my results were quite abnormal. He stated that I was suffering from bradicardia, slow heart rate, and arrhythmia, irregular heartbeat. He was very taken aback by these findings on such a young and vibrant lady. He wanted me to wear a halter heart monitor for the next twenty-four hours. He also called a friend of his who was a Psychiatrist and asked him questions about the medicines that I was taking. The jackpot answer came when his colleague reported that the symptoms my heart was exhibiting were the same as side effects from the drug, Lithium. When Dr. Snapper told us this, then I thought that he would take me off the klonopin which trigged these side effects. I had been on lithium for two years without any heart problems. But Dr. Snapper decided to keep me on the klonopin and stop the Lithium. Of course, we called Dr. RB about all of this, and he promptly concurred with Dr. Snapper. Over the next twenty-four hours, I wore the heart monitor constantly as I had been instructed to do. After the twenty-four hours were up, and I had stopped the Lithium, I was already beginning to notice a difference. I went back the next day to have the halter monitor removed and to find out the results. The nurse took the test out of the room and started to throw them away because she thought that the monitor had messed up. We had a different nurse this time who was not familiar with the bizarre antics of my heart. When Dr. Snapper asked her for the results, she said, "Oh, I threw them away; the results were inaccurate." Dr. Snapper jumped after the trash can exclaiming to everyone in sight that those results were, indeed, accurate! Upon retrieval of the test papers, Dr. Snapper stared in amazement as he studied the results. On a regular basis, my heart rate was forty beats per minute, and when I felt the head rush, my heart rate dropped to twenty beats per minute! Dr. Snapper was completely dumbfounded! How I survived during those few weeks that my heart was under this duress is still a mystery to us all. The fact that I was continuing on with my regular activities, which included jogging, and the fact that I didn't collapse, is a miracle itself. I realized after this ordeal, that God definitely wanted me around to raise my three girls!

Now that the Lithium had been removed from my diet and the klonopin, was working, my health continued to improve. The klonopin was very effective in eliminating the anxiety and panic attacks that had controlled my life for nearly three years. At this point, Dr. RB continued to fine tune my chemicals and I continued to gradually piece all the fragments of my life back together again. I was, now, pretty much in control of my life. I could drive just about anywhere, and I was able to take care of the kids and run the house by myself. Regardless of how in control I was, Mark still kept a nanny/house keeper around through all these years. We had a new nanny now, named Valerie, who took over when Vicki left to get married and raise her own family. We were always fortunate to have good people work for us and keep us afloat during the good times and the bad.

Over the next three years, our lives were getting back in order, and we were happily functioning on our own again. One thing that Dr. RB continued to try was to reduce my medicines. Every time he scaled back on one medicine, then I would start slipping backward again. So, for the meantime, Dr. RB, Mark and I, all decided to give everything more time. I still had little areas of concern when placed in certain situations that would typically unnerve me, but for the most part, I was doing well. One of the main areas that I struggled with was the fact that I could drive anywhere on the surface streets without fear of any kind, but the highway were a different story. The problem with the highways or expressways was the fear I had of encountering a panic attack and having no real place of refuge. Obviously, the emergency lanes provide ample space for such an occurrence, however, that opportunity doesn't provide comfort to the individual driving under the influence of a panic attack. Once a panic attack occurs, the person experiencing the attack cannot afford to think rationally. It's virtually impossible to get control over the shock-induced chemical alterations of the brain that have taken over. Another reason that the expressways caused a problem was that they provided too much wide open spacing on the road. It was the same problem that I initially had during the early phase of the healing process with the wide open spaces of the grocery stores and the long narrow aisles within them. Once again, panic attacks are not welcome foes on any turf. Experiencing an attack is similar to a person suffering from shock usually due to some type of serious injury; only the victim of a panic attack is not physically injured. The God-given purpose for this chemical response is to ensure survival by the "fight or flight" response when our lives are in danger. What happens with a panic disorder is that the fight or flight response is in overload and its trigger happy. Needless to say, I stayed off the major roadways for many years. Also, unbelievably, I had the fear of flying on an airplane. Imagine that, a former flight attendant, afraid of flying. I wasn't afraid of the typical things that most people fear like mechanical failure and such. I was afraid of one thing . . . having a panic attack. First of all, on an airplane, you can't get off instantly if you do suffer an attack. Secondly, I would be totally embarrassed to show that behavior in front of other people. And, finally, there was no escape. If I couldn't get away to my "happy place," then I felt that I would continue to panic into oblivion. The mere thought of it paralyzed me with fear. And that's exactly what anxiety is . . . paralysis by fear. Since I was happy with my abilities to function as I was, then I didn't rock the boat by pushing myself to do things that I didn't feel confident doing. With that, my family and I continued on merrily with our lives. We were happy, content, and together again as a family unit. This lifestyle is the way we predicted the future would continue for us, however, the best and the worst was yet to come.

Chapter Five

A Fork in the Road

Five years had passed since the initial trauma of my illness had imposed on my family and me, and we were all finally enjoying life as it should be. The baby, Jordan, had just entered Kindergarten, and I was looking forward to a more relaxed lifestyle since all three girls were now in school. Since I am somewhat of a neat freak, I had devised a plan to, first and foremost, clean out all the clutter in the house and organize everything perfectly. After that undertaking, I had plans to visit Barnes & Noble on a regular basis and read books all day while sipping a nice, refreshing Frapachino! That's the life that I had envisioned for myself and one that I truly planned on carrying out. Of course, before any of these dreams could come true, I first had to finish the wash!

Another important piece of the puzzle that needed great attention in order to completely put our future on the right course was that of permanent sterilization for one of us. We were certain that our baby bearing years were over, and I considered myself to be incapable of having another baby. I sort of blacklisted myself with this term because not only did I suffer severely with the depression, but I also had endured three C-sections. Those two factors alone were plenty reason enough to call it quits for us in the baby industry. This was a very big decision for us, since we both knew that my baby bearing years were over. Actually, two years after having Jordan, Mark and I met with Dr. Schilling, and discussed the procedure of a tubule ligation for me. However, at that time, I was very fearful of having any procedure done due to the fact that I was still dealing with a fragile and unpredictable state of mind. I was fearful that the use of anesthesia and other drugs would upset the delicate condition of my mind and possibly set me back. Dr. Schilling explained the entire procedure but I couldn't find enough comfort in his words to believe that I should have the procedure done at this time. Three years later, I still thought about going through with that surgery, but something told me that I needed to leave my body alone. On the other hand, Mark had no intentions, what so ever, to mess with the "family jewels" as he put it. I've learned that that there are two types of men, those that can't wait to jump into the surgery chair and have the vasectomy done, and those that run far away from ever doing such a thing. There's no middle ground when it comes to men and vasectomies. I've found another correlation that runs similar with women. There are two kinds of women, those that love breast feeding and those that loathe the thought of it. Once again, there is no gray area when it comes to this subject matter. With my decision to leave my body alone, and Mark's abstinence about a vasectomy, we simply stayed with our regular form of birth control. The main concern was not convenience, but sterility. We felt comfortable that we were safe with our present form of protection.

During this period of embellishment as we were blissfully enjoying our family life, I would often join the girls at lunch at school. Eating lunch at the table with a bunch of elementary kids, who have little or no concern for manners, can be quite interesting at times. One day, while I was lunching with Jamie, her teacher informed me that she had written out her Christmas list, and that she stated on the bottom of her list a wish for her mother to have twin baby girls. I said, "Oh, aren't you people funny!" Not only did the teacher relish with delight at telling me this, she also decided to display Jamie's Christmas wish list on the hallway outside her room for God and everyone to see! I smirking smiled and laughed at the teacher's delight in mocking me and joking at my expense. The teacher and I were great friends, so she knew all too well how I felt about having another baby. The reality of the situation was that at times I did feel that I could handle raising another baby, but I knew that I couldn't handle another pregnancy. Sometimes I felt that there was more to our family than we knew. Even though these thoughts crossed my mind form time to time, I knew we were done having children. Another interesting point about Jamie listing twin girls on her Christmas list was that Jamie always loved playing with twin dolls. All during Jamie's early childhood she made her toys into twin everything. Even her one of her birthday cakes had twin mermaids on the top of it! I told Jamie, that when she grew up, that she would one day have twins. Not only do I still believe that she will have twins, but twins run in my family. Anyway, I loved her Christmas list even if it did involve twin baby girls and me.

Shortly after the holidays when the girls returned to school, we had our first experience with one of the kids coming home with head lice! It proved to be the nightmare that all parents fear. I started treating Jamie with the regular over the counter treatments that were recommended by her pediatrician. We did the treatments by day, and combed her hair thoroughly in the mornings picking out all of the nits. Oh, what a fun routine to repeat day and night. Jamie would tear up in frustration at how long the constant combing and picking took. After several treatments and weeks of frustration dealing with this, I contacted the school to voice my frustration with the school about the policy on kids coming to school with head lice and exposing other kids. The failure of the treatments to work and the constant agony that Jamie was enduring, lead me to question the school on why she was exposed to lice in the first place. Not only did I contact the school, but I contacted the Henry County Health Department and Jamie's doctor about other treatments. After much research and "gnashing of teeth," I contacted an organization up north called the National Pediculosis Association. It was comprised of mothers, like me, who had lengthy struggles treating head lice. They were very reassuring and helpful with their solutions. I bought several videos from them and pamphlets about their treatments and their effectiveness. The solution was as basic as it was simple; the cure for head lice was . . . olive oil. Olive oil has been the treatment of choice since the ancient times when it was discovered for its true purposes in Israel. The procedure was to soak your child's head in the olive oil at night and cover the head with a shower cap. The child sleeps in the shower cap, and in the morning, after you comb the hair and pick the nits, you then wash the child's hair with a degreasing, dishwashing soap like Dawn. After the hair has been degreased, then you wash the child's hair with regular shampoo to give the hair a softer texture. Once that procedure is complete, then your child can go to school without being contagious or obvious to any other students. The olive oil is full proof because it completely smothers the lice and their nits. This process needs to be repeated every other night for two weeks and then head lice are gone completely! The traditional treatments that we had started with at the local drug store are becoming less effective because the head lice are becoming more resistant to those chemicals. It's the same as people taking too many antibiotics. After a while, the bacteria become resistant to the antibiotic, resulting in more problems for doctors and their patients. Obviously, I've studied and researched this information quite a bit. When you're a mother looking for solutions to your child's condition, then you become a researcher of many aliments and illness that affect your children, and by the time you're finished raising them, then you could have the knowledge of a registered nurse! No wonder grandparents are so wise and enjoy their grandchildren so much.

Also, initial treating the lice problem meant that I also had to treat the family and myself with the approved medications recommended by the school. Five weeks after Jamie had contracted the bugs, Jordan, also, came down with the devious little critters, but by this time I had learned of the olive oil treatment, and used it effectively on her and Jamie. Since my life had been preoccupied with treating the entire family and house for lice, I had given up my routine of jogging everyday. Needless to say, I was completely swamped with overwhelming chores trying to chemically blast all predators from the house and presumably the planet!

The house treatment for lice is just as invasive as the scalp treatment is. First, all the sheets on all the beds had to be sterilized in the wash which accumulated to thirteen loads of wash a day. All bed comforters were sent out to the dry cleaners as were sofa pillows and the like. Next, the new housekeeper, Valerie, and I bagged up all the "gazillions" of stuffed animals and put them away for two weeks. It was a long and arduous process, but we kept at it. By the time that I felt comfortable opening the decontaminated comforters from their wrap and placing them back on the beds, then Jamie would walk in the room scratching her head, and we start the whole process over again! It was during this time that I realized that I needed to resort to a familiar commodity from my past and do as my mother had done raising her brood of eleven, and I did so by informing Mark that we needed to invest in two more laundry machine; a washer and a dryer. People thought that I was crazy, but it was a normal concept for me since I had been raise in that manner. I didn't have eleven kids' clothes to wash, but three still proved plenty of work especially when it comes to unforeseen emergencies like head lice.

During all the commotion of treating the lice epidemic in the house, I hadn't had time to engage in my regular routine of exercise of jogging. Now that we had the lice problem under control, I was fully ready to lunge back into exercise and work off some built-up frustration. Part of that frustration was that I was beginning to notice that my pants were getting tight around my abdomen and my muscles were getting loose. Also, it was time for my annual exam with Dr. Schilling and my regular mammogram. Since there was a history of breast cancer in my family, the doctor suggested that I have mammograms regularly starting in my thirties. The day arrived when I was to attend my appointment with Dr. Schilling for the gynecological check-up and the "Breast Nazi" for the "boob lock-down." I started off with the mammogram first, and the clinician asked me when my last period was. I gave her the date and told her that I was due any minute with my next one. After I got through with the machine that turned my voluptuous breast into a pair of flat pancakes, then I was ready and willing to see the doctor for my next poking and prodding session. You got to love those annual check ups! Well, everything checked out fine, and I went on my merry way.

A few days after my appointment at Dr. Schilling's office, I became curious that I had not started my cycle yet. Sometimes I run late with my periods anyway, so I wasn't alarmed. As the days past, I began to experience some more, interesting symptoms that I had known well in the past. I couldn't quite figure out what was going on with these unusual signs that my body was encountering. Over the next weekend, my friend Sheree and I took the kids to the Fabulous Fox Theatre to see the *Rug Rats* Show on stage. During the show, I kept having menstrual like cramps but no period occurred. After my last visit to the restroom, I knew something was up. I greatly sensed that I was, pregnant! I wanted so badly to confide in Sheree and tell her of my suspicions, but I wanted to be sure first before I said anything to anybody, including my best friend. I didn't even say anything to Mark. Later that night, Mark and I had dinner with his mother and her friend, Joan. For some strange reason, I was paranoid about the food that I was eating. I wanted to make sure the chicken was cooked enough. I made Mark scrutinize the piece of meat carefully and with great detail. This was not my normal behavior. It was like something was taking over me and controlling my thoughts and actions. The kicker came the next day when we attended church, and I was sitting in Sunday school drinking my morning coffee. I looked down and noticed that my fingers were swollen. Not only that, but the coffee didn't taste right either. As I became more convinced, by the minute, that I was pregnant, I also became more panicked about the true possibility! Our Sunday school teacher that day was Jay Dockweiler, and he taught a very compelling message that hit home with me right away. His lesson for the day was the story of Joseph and Mary as they journeyed through her pregnancy with Jesus, and how both of them must have felt in their predicament, but how they followed through with God's plan for their lives. I listened intently as I knew that God had Jay deliver that message for all of us, but it processed special meaning for me that day. God knew what was coming for Mark and me, and he was preparing us for the road ahead.

After class was over, Mark and I met with our best friends, Fran and Al

Harrell, in the hallway. I didn't realize it at the time, but apparently I was acting strange to them and Fran later told me how jittery I seemed, and how she thought that I was being somewhat snobby. I know that I was anxious, but snobby? We left church to go eat at one of our favorite restaurants, the farmer's market, in College Park. I always loved their breakfasts and I always indulged in the sausage and eggs with another cup of coffee. As I looked forward to my meal again on this day, once again, ordering my favorite hearty breakfast, I was quickly dismayed at the taste of the food. It didn't taste right, nor did it taste the same as it always had which was quite disappointing for me. It was just another reminder, that I was most likely pregnant. On the way home, I finally told Mark my suspicions and suggested to him that we stop at the local drug store and get a pregnancy test. He happily obliged me with a cute, smirk on his face as he said, "There's no way that you could be pregnant." Famous last words! I walked in the store hoping that no one would notice me while I was buying the test, and as quickly as I slipped in the store, I slipped out the door and headed home to test my luck

Once at home, I hurried to the bathroom to do the test while Mark waited curiously in the bedroom to hear the verdict. After I did the test, I laid the stick on the bathroom floor and waited the allotted amount of time to check the window for the presence or absence of the little, pink line. At first, I didn't see anything, and I was greatly relieved, but then something caught my eye, and I looked again at the small window which revealed a thin, faint line of . . . pink.

I walked into the bedroom, where Mark was sitting, waiting for "Dr. Connie" to perform her own pregnancy test, and in the same breath that I uttered the words, positive, to him; the atmosphere around us began to change as we realized our guarded and confusing news would soon endure the test of time. Anytime a couple finds out that they are expecting a baby, it's usually a happy time as it had always been for us, so a certain amount of joy did seep into our hearts and minds, however, it was quickly overshadowed with great concerns about the obvious, health issues. We kept the news to ourselves that Sunday and decided on a plan to follow the at-home pregnancy test with the official test at Dr. Schilling's office the very next day. I felt pretty good that day; so somehow, Mark and I went about our usual business for a Sunday trying not to dwell on the situation until we had more information. That night, I sat down on the sofa with the girls to watch a movie, and as I was sitting there with all three of them curled up around me, I felt somewhat of a premonition that this could very possibly be the last time that I would enjoy such a peaceful moment with my family. Somehow, I must have sensed that the ship on which I was riding was about to encounter a storm of great magnitude!

As soon as I got the girls off to school, I was on the phone with my doctor's office requesting an appointment for a pregnancy test that morning. The receptionist, who answered my call, was not the least bit concerned about scheduling a routing pregnancy test for me that morning. She seemed to be quite clinical in her approach to handling endless phones calls from women requesting regular pregnancy tests. Once I clearly defined to her that this was not an ordinary situation then, she started to pay attention. I told her that this was a complicated issue due to the fact that I had three previous C-sections, a serious history with postpartum depression and was currently taking four psychiatric medications! She appeared more interested in my declaration after she got an earful of all that.

Pam Garrett, a physician's assistant (PA), was the only attending clinician for the day as everyone else was scheduled for surgery. I had known Pam for years and was greatly relieved that she was the one on call. The receptionist told me to come on in and let Pam perform the pregnancy test. Pam greeted me with high spirits and her usual calm and fun-loving demeanor as she approached me, and then she proceeded on with the test. The results came quickly, and there was no doubt about it. I was pregnant! After she and I realized the gravity of the situation, she took me into an examining room for a physical, and she found that everything looked fine. Pam knew all too well my history with post-partum depression and the number of surgeries that I had already experienced, but she remained very encouraging with the words of wisdom that she provided me that day. She made me feel that this pregnancy was a very doable deal which helped to release some of the negative worries that had already started to build in my mind. We exchanged positive conversation after the exam was over, and I left her office with a hopeful outlook on the pregnancy. Immediately, I left her office, and headed straight to Mark's office to give him the confirmation of the news. He smiled, and then answered a phone call that had just come in. Once he realized that the person on the other end of the phone was his friend, Al Harrell, he quoted Ben Affleck in the movie, *Good Will Hunting,* by asking Al if he liked apples. When Al said, "Yes, I like apples," Mark said, "Well Connie's pregnant; how do you like them apples?" And that's how we began the introduction to the world that we were expecting the unexpected!

I left Mark's office and headed straight to our local pharmacy, Eagle's Landing Pharmacy, to buy some "big sister" buttons for the girls to wear. After making that purchase, then I proceeded to the elementary school to treat the girls with the big news by bringing them the buttons to wear. Before I entered the school building, I placed the very necessary call in to Dr. RB's office to inform him of this interesting predicament that had befall The voice mail came on at his office, so I proceeded to leave an upbeat message since my mood at the time was confident and positive. I then entered the school building and signed in at the office while informing all the office staff that I was taking the big sister buttons to each of the girls in their respective classrooms. The entire office staff went crazy over the news because they knew us well, but they didn't know of all the trouble that I usually had with pregnancies. I just pretended that everything was normal, and then I headed off to each girl's rooms to break the news. I started with Jackie first, knocked on the door and asked her to come to the door. As she cheerfully greeted me at the door, I explained that Mommy was going to have another baby and that she was going to be a big sister again! She was excited, but she mostly seemed to be in a state of shock. I hugged her, sent her back to class with her new button for all to see, and then I walked on to the other girls' rooms and repeated the same process over again. Each of the girls responded in the same manner as Jackie did by staring in amazement and gleefully smiling at the news. As I returned them to their rooms, their smiles remained frozen on their faces. After officially breaking the news to the girls, I headed back to the car and found that Dr. RB had left a message. I quickly returned his phone call, and he stated that he wanted to see Mark and me in his office the very next day. We set up the appointment right away and agreed that this was an urgent matter.

The next day, Tuesday, Mark and I were scheduled to take Mark's mom to the airport for her flight to Memphis to visit her sister, Marie. On the way there, she excitedly talked about the upcoming addition to the family and wondered if we might have twins this time around. Since twins run in my family, the possibility for that occurrence was very real, and ironically, I had allowed the same thought to pass through my mind. Later in the pregnancy, we would find that many people shared the same intuition, but as Pam Garrett said, on my initial visit with her, "God would not do that to you." As we drove to the airport and discussed the impending pregnancy with Mark's Mom, I noticed that my mood was starting to change. My mind was drifting backward to a familiar place that I knew all too well and feared more than death itself. A grey cloud was looming toward me bringing with it a feeling of doom and desperation. It startled me to realize that I was beginning to feel a wave of depression roll over me while I was still under the influence of the same four psychiatric medicines that had kept me afloat over the past five years. I couldn't imagine, in my worst nightmare, that I could ever experience the feeling of depression again especially while taking four proven medicines. I knew that I was in trouble, and I was scared of what the future of this predicament would hold for us.

Later that afternoon we arrived at DR. RB's office ready to discuss the issue at hand and to determine the plan for the next nine plus months. Upon meeting Dr. RB we conversed with our usual greetings and polite talk before getting into the significant subject matter at hand. Soon afterward though, as we delved further into the matter, Mark and I both let down our guard and confessed all our concerns and dilemmas in facing such an astonishing feat. I cried hysterically at the thought of jeopardizing our future with the girls that we already had, and Mark released his pent up guilt for allowing this to happen. We knew we were in for a tough, uphill battle, and we looking to Dr. RB to be our God, our guide and our leader. And he did just that. Just when we thought that all hope was gone, Dr. RB came through with an ingenious plan. And that's what we needed at the time . . . a plan. I guess that since this pregnancy wasn't planned, we forgot that we could take control of our lives by implementing a plan. We sat quietly and listened intently as Dr. RB explained the game plan, and with each soothing word that he spoke, our fears dissipated and our hopes returned.

The first thing that he instructed us to do was for me to start reducing my medicines that very night in a sequential order that would continue over the next four days until I was completely off all the medicines. Now this is the kicker, Dr. RB stated that I might feel a little "funky" during this process. At the time that he mentioned the word funky, I didn't think anything substantial about the word. I had felt funky plenty of times before with all the incredible episodes that I had endured in the past, so this word did not particularly alarm me. Dr. RB continued to explain all the different, possible scenarios that we could find ourselves in as we traveled these un-chartered waters, but he had an answer for all of them also, so we left his office feeling relieved and uplifted by the words he had spoken. We ensued with our ritualistic, date-night dinner afterward where we continued to soak up the instructions and advice that we had been given. We amazed ourselves at the optimistic attitude that we had both just adopted from the doctor, and we were fortunate to enjoy a brief moment of hope and joy about the future.

Once we arrived home, I began the new prescribed method of treatment right away and only took the allowed medicines before heading to bed. As I lay in bed cautiously optimistic about the future, I struggled to fall asleep. It was becoming quite apparent to me that the lack of one pill from my regular routine of nightly medicines was already having a substantial effect on me. I finally drifted off to sleep somewhere around two o'clock in the morning and awoke to the screaming alarm clock at six o'clock am to get up with the kids for school. That morning was pretty much routine for the kids and me, so I dared not show any signs of sleep deprivation. After I dropped the kids off at school, I headed back home to start a day's worth of housework. Other than the lack of sleep, I didn't suffer any other ramifications of illness throughout the day. However mentally healthy I felt at the time, an old pregnancy symptom of my previous pregnancies came back for a forth and final victory run in the form of nausea. As most women who experience nausea during pregnancy know, it's not a morning event; it's an all day affair! There are few words that can describe the sometimes incapacitating, and constant flow of hormone induced nausea that changes every aspect of the digestive system including the altercation of the taste of food from fabulous to offensive. Since nausea had always accompanied all of my other pregnancies, so it wasn't surprising nor inviting to encounter its return this time.

As night two rolled around, I feared the worst and hoped for the best as far as sleep would go. However, it was not to be, and I tossed and turned for hours on end. The "Sand Man" didn't come visit until the "wee" hour of four in the morning. The next day, I functioned well for a sleep deprived, nauseated, pregnant mother of three children carrying out her duties for the day. Other than the sleep deprivation, I was feeling very good mentally and physically. I was pleased with the progress that I was making while weaning off the four medications, and I had every reason to believe that I could function well without the use of medicines. However, the changes that were beginning to take place would soon take a bigger and unexpected toll on me than either Mark or I could have imagined.

As the insomnia held me captive all during the third night, I struggled endlessly trying to find some way to induce the sleep. I finally got up to change the scenery in hopes of better luck. Not only did I hope that a change in venue could possibly help, but in the bedroom, I hung onto every sigh of breath that Mark inhaled during his blissful, nocturnal sleep, and it resonated through my head until I couldn't take it anymore. Once I moved into the den and took up residency on the sofa, I noticed another bothersome noise in the form of the tick-tock from the wall clock located near the den. If I couldn't tolerate Mark's breathing, then surely the clock ticking would prove to be more of a disturbing foe. So, I proceeded to remove the clock from the wall in order to silence its effects. I lay back down on the sofa, and again I heard the tick-tock! I grew furious and frustrated at the continuing annoyance, so I tried again to silence the noise. Finally, I realized that by laying the clock flat on the ground, the noise would stop and so would the clock. I didn't care that I had stopped the clock; I just wanted silence and sleep. I thought, "In the morning, Mark's going to wonder what in the world happened to the clock during the night." I figured I'd explain it in the morning, and hopefully he wouldn't think that I was completely crazy!

On that third night, I finally began to drift off into a restless sleep at five o'clock in the morning, and I awoke before the alarm sounded at six o'clock. Physically, I was numb and lifeless. I called out to Mark and asked him if he could go upstairs and get the kids ready for school. After he did that, he came over came over to me and tried to massage my body in order to provide some comfort and relief for me, but it did nothing. I could move my limbs, but my nerve endings would not respond to any stimuli. I could have paid the best massage therapist in the world for a soothing massage, but it still would not have any affect on my diminishing, tactile reflexes. I was now officially miserable. After the girls left for school that day, I proceeded to get up and pull myself together for the day's events. I just held on the best I could trying to keep some semblance of myself and my life. Everything around me seemed to be fading away, and I was fading away with it.

The fourth night came and went just like the three previous ones had providing little rest for the weary. On Friday morning, I got up and readied the girls for school. Mark drove them to school and then returned home to check on me. As he entered, I was moving very slowly from the kitchen, where I had retrieved some saltine crackers to help with the impending nausea, to the den to sit in the recliner and stare at the morning news. Mark joined me in the den and sat down on the sofa next to me while I tried to nimble away on the saltines. I became anxious at the strange feelings that were beginning to engulf me, and I asked Mark to stay until I felt better. He had a meeting waiting for him at the office, but he agreed to stay. The peculiar feelings became more invasive by the moment and fear ran rampant throughout my body and soul. While these changes were coming over me, I talked to Mark about my ability to go through the pregnancy. He reassured me that I could make it through all these complications and that things would soon get better. As we talked further about our situation my voice started weakening and my ability to speak was drifting away. With every utterance of each word that I attempted to speak, my voice faded away into obscurity, and simultaneously my mind and body were vacuumed up into a tunnel of oblivion. At the same time that my voice started to go, my entire body began to shake, and every part of me was physically and literally going numb. The numbness reached every morsel of my body to the point that I could not feel the saltine cracker sitting on my tongue! It was as if I was being swept up into a dark and dangerous funnel cloud and being lead towards the twilight zone. As my existence shifted beyond my comprehension, I briefly floated away as if I were listening to "ground control attempt contact with Major Tom" in the lyrics to the song, *Space Odyssey,* by David Bowie. My life was suspended in the abyss of this mysterious fate.

As quickly as this peculiar spell had come over me; . . . it left. I couldn't believe it. All of a sudden, I felt like a new person. It was as if my body had been processed by some foreign invader, and needed to flush it out. Not only was I elated that this wacky phenomenon had passed, but I was completely astonished that I suddenly felt fantastic! It was incredible how bizarre this entire experience had been. One minute I felt as if I were suspended in space, and the next minute, I'm back on planet earth talking normally with my husband! After I gained my composure, I gave Mark permission to leave. Relieved himself that my condition had improved, he relinquished his babysitting duties and headed to the office. Shortly after he left, the door bell rang, and I went to answer it. Greeting me at the door, in was my long time friend and confidant, Susie Grant. I was so surprised to see her because we didn't visit each other on a regular basis due to our hectic schedules. We would usually make plans to get together, or we would run into each other during the course of the day. I was thrilled to see her and hopeful that she wouldn't notice any signs from my previous encounter. We sat and had a nice visit which was therapeutic because she helped further the course that I had begun back into the world of normalcy. After her visit, I proceeded to get my shower and get started on with my day.

Over the next few days, I felt descent during the day with a slight infraction of anxiety or sadness mixed in upon occasion. But I still couldn't sleep more than two hours at night. This problem continued to grow into a dreadful monster. Anyone who has ever suffered from insomnia knows how horrible it is to live with and how detrimental it can be to your emotional health. At night, I would just lay there tossing and turning with no relief in sight. I also started to have the nausea that comes with pregnancy, at eleven o'clock at night along with the insomnia! Now this was a fun mixture! No sleep mixed with nausea was a combination that I hadn't experienced before. I could never have dreamed of such a deplorable nightmare. I struggled and I struggled at night. Negative thoughts entered my head, and I felt like I was all alone in the world. I lay in bed terrified at night seeing myself as some kind of monster. Not only were things not going well for me, but I felt guilty that I was always sick. My negative thoughts made me feel like I was a bad person. I didn't feel loved, and I didn't love myself. I would day dream at night that I would miscarry, and that this whole, horrible nightmare, that I was living, would be gone. I would endure thoughts like that, and then I'd try to eat another saltine cracker to curb the nausea.

Not only was I suffering at night, but my days were also becoming uncomfortable with mixes of anxiety and depression swooning in to complete the entire recipe of disaster that had become my life. During the day I was also dealing with the increase in the nausea, so eating and having a good appetite were more of the pleasures that were being stripped away from me. I couldn't eat, sleep or enjoy life. I remember one particular Saturday morning I sat down on the sofa to join the family watching television, and I started thumbing through the "new mom" bag that I received at the doctor's office. I tried to look through it to draw some inspiration and regain some purpose for my life. All I discovered as I browsed the magazine was the feeling, been there, done that. While I sat there looking for some form of symbolism of happiness, I was beginning to feel anxiety winding up in my head to a level of uncomfortable proportions. Mark decided that it would be a good idea for the family to get out during the day and have an adventure. So, we decided to venture all the way down to Locust Grove to Tanger Outlet Mall, to shop for some clothes for me to grow into. The pressure of the anxiety and depression was going at full speed now, as I dressed for our outing. I was falling deeper and deeper into the bottomless pit of Hades. I continued to fight the onset of symptoms while I continued to ready myself to get out. One of the kids came running in from outside the house screaming that she was all of a sudden scared and for no reason. As mothers usually do, I hid my own fears in order to comfort her. I thought to myself, "What's going on here? Are we under attack? Can things get much worse?" Well, the answer to all of those questions was . . . yes! We finally all loaded up in the car and headed to Tanger On the way there, I had such horrible, somewhat psychotic episodes, in my head where I thought bizarre things about myself and my family. These thoughts were horrible and tragic. The thoughts that bombarded my mind were incomprehensible! It was like living in a demonic nightmare where my worst fears appeared to be a reality show unfolding before my very own eyes. To compound the problem, I felt as if I were some wicked, evil monster for allowing these thoughts to even come into my head. For a while I couldn't escape the haunting, torment that these thoughts possessed over me. I didn't tell Mark my thoughts, at that time, but I did say to him, "When I die and go to heaven, then none of this will be with me will it?" Mark just reassured me that everything would be fine. We went on with our shopping trip, and I worked to "will" myself out of this deplorable predicament. After a while of walking and browsing the stores, I did start to recover to some degree, but I was still very depressed. The evil thoughts finally began to subside, and I was starting to feel some relief from the constant pain. Once we were finished with our errands, we finally headed back home pleased that we had a bit of a successful trip. Once home, I sat down in the play room to watch *Peter Pan* with the kids. I never have liked that movie, and today was no exception. The part of the movie where

Peter Pan and all the kids fight the lost boys depresses me even on a good day.

Later that night, Dr. RB returned my urgent phone call that I had placed to him earlier in the day. He first apologized for calling so late, but his phone had been down, and he had just gotten it back to working. I talked to him with Mark on the other end of the phone listening as I explained my horrors of the day. Dr. RB had a way of taking the worse case scenarios and turning them into a happy place. He made a suggestion about medicine, and decided to put me back on trilafon. He said that would ease up the depression and it would also treated those intrusive thoughts that I was having. He'd told me before about those intrusive thoughts stating that I'm not some psycho killer, but that the thoughts come from the subconsciencous, and they are really my worst fears. Anything that I would fear the most, is what surfaces under the duress of my mental challenges at the time. Somehow, in the midst of the conversation, I found myself laughing. How that was possible, I do not know. I wasn't laughing hysterically as in some psychotic phase, but I was feeling better in a genuine way and discovered that life isn't always that serious. The ability to laugh is the best medicine and the best indicator that everything is going to be fine. I started back on the trilafon that night, and for the first time in weeks I slept through the night! As each day went by, I continued to improve until I was back functioning in a normal fashion. Needless to say, it was a welcome relief.

Now, all I had to do was deal with the constant morning sickness. It can be so incapacitating! The hormones changes that occur while pregnant alter your taste buds in your mouth. Food doesn't taste the same, and every bite tempts a regurgitation response if the food doesn't settle well. It may not sound like that big of a deal to others, but it affects every part of you, and it greatly affects how you feel. It's hard to keep up a happy disposition when you feel your stomach in your throat all day long. Anyway, I had dealt with it on all the other pregnancies, so I would learn to deal with it during this one. Other than that, things were going smoothly, and I was thrilled to be happy again! I had still been cleaning up from the aftermath of the head lice ordeal, so I was still busy cleaning house and getting things back in order. Between that and keeping up with the kids, I may have been overdoing things a little. One day, a friend of mine, Sherry Thomason, came by to pick me up for Bible Study. My car was in the shop, so she offered me a ride. Boy, does God know what he's doing while we sit idle by thinking we have things under control? The answer is . . . yes! I had no idea what was about to happen that day! During Bible Study, I joked and jested with all the other ladies as I was joyful to be out of the house and away from the constant thought of how uncomfortable this pregnancy was. I remarked that I couldn't wait until I reached menopause. What a relief that would be! They all thought that I had lost my mind. I told them, "No, actually, I already did that!" We had a great Bible Study, and it was so refreshing to hear the written word from the Bible. Bible Study always gave me such a lift. It takes me away from the everyday dread of all the bad things going on in the world and puts me at peace in the hand of the Father. This day was no exception. After the study was over, I waited for Sherry to finish things up and give me a ride home. Only this time, I decided to call Mark and ask him out to lunch. He graciously accepted my offer, and Sherry and I would head to his office where she would drop me off. Before I left the house, I made my usual visit to the restroom. Then, I was ready to go. The minute that I sat down in Sherry's car, I felt something very strange happen. It felt like I had just accidentally pushed out some urine in my pants. It thought how strange that could be since I had just gone to the bathroom. It took Sherry a few minutes to reach the car, and I became more nervous with each passing minute. It was a very short drive to Mark's office, but it felt like it was forever away. Once she dropped me off, I briefly looked down at my seat to make sure that I hadn't left any surprises there. I quickly rushed into Mark's office and headed straight to the bathroom. Once I sat down, I knew something terrible had happened. I had a huge pool of blood all in my underwear and pants! I was continuing to bleed in the toilet. I pulled things together as quickly as I could and headed out the door to find someone who might have a pad. The first person I encountered pleasingly obliged. I thought that her reaction was so calm, because pregnant women don't usually ask for a pad! After I secured things, I alerted Mark with the news, and in a flash, we were headed off to the hospital! Thankfully, in the towns of McDonough and Stockbridge, everything was close by, including the hospital. In fact, it was located just across the street from Mark's office. As we approached the emergency room, we were in conversation on the phone, with Dr. Schilling's office. They promised us that they would page him right away. I entered the emergency room by myself since Mark dropped me off to park the car. There was no absolute desk with a receptionist at it that signaled the place for me to go. So, I just walked around until someone said, "May I help you?" And I responded, "Yes, I'm having a miscarriage." Well, that got things going! A nurse took me into a room and started with all the applicable questions and procedures. She started with my blood pressure while she asked me questions. I was a little concerned that my blood pressure was much higher than normal for me. I'm usually at 100/60 and it was 135/80. I assured myself that it was just from the stress of the situation. They quickly got me situated in a room, and mark joined me there. I got dressed in the Victoria Secret style gown that we've all come to love at the hospital and settled into my bed. Mark and I talked over the situation and how it all got started. I told him that I was so looking forward to lunch with him that day because my appetite was coming back. I was at thirteen weeks pregnancy, so that's sometimes the appropriate time for the nausea to cut off. Finally, a doctor came in to see me. Mark and I took a good, long hard look at this young intern realizing that this *kid* was no match for me. Right in the middle of his questioning me on the problem at hand, God walked in! Not really, it was just Dr. Schilling, but, at that time, he was God! He sent the poor, little intern back to his duties which came with a great sigh of relief from the intern and us. Dr. Schilling came in with his usual, jovial self, asking me, "What's going on?" I told him the entire story, and he first wanted to do an ultrasound. He asked if I had anymore bleeding since the first gush, and I told him, amazingly, "No." He said that we would do nothing until we had an ultrasound. I was wheeled in to the ultrasound room and met the clinician. He did "his thing" with the ultrasound and away we went. Surprisingly enough, not only did we have a heartbeat, but the baby was doing the Macarena dance! Dr. Schilling surmised that I had probably suffered a ruptured blood vessel, and he ordered me to bed rest for two weeks. I asked, "like, so, how much housework can I do?" He said, "None, bed rest means bed rest!" He told me that could sit during the day on the sofa, so that I wouldn't be completely confined to bed. I wasn't sure about how I would make it for two weeks on bed rest. I'm not the sitting kind of person. I'm a busy girl! Well, that was doctor's orders, so I had to commit myself to it. I thought how ironic it was that I was almost finished with a great book that I had started reading a couple of months before, and now I was almost finished with it. This would be the perfect time to start a book that was as good as this one. I also thought about occupying my time with some basic needle point work and other fun artistic crafts.

Mark made me lunch when we arrived home, and now the appetite that I had before, was now leaving me. I was back to the good old nausea with food tasting plain. I assumed, from my medical and professional point of view, that the reason my stomach was feeling great before, was because my hormones may have reduced, during the stress of the bleeding episode, leaving me vulnerable to a miscarriage. It was shocking to understand how close we possibly came to the finality of the pregnancy when we had no concept that the pregnancy could be that fragile. We had never before encountered a problem like this one during the previous, three pregnancies. Once the kids got home from school, we decided to tell them only pertinent information about what happened, so they would understand why Mom was on bed rest.

I wasn't looking forward to the bed rest because not only am I a naturally busy person, but busy work helps to pass time. Sitting all day makes each day feel like an eternity. I dreaded every minute that passed by. The days were long and extremely boring. My biggest fear was that after this phase was over, that I could possibly undergo another set back and repeat the process all over again. I just, simply didn't think that I could face that again or endure it either. Several friends called with words of comfort to cheer me up, and it all helped a good bit, but, I still couldn't help feeling isolated from the rest of the world. Pregnancy, itself, is quite a challenge to live with for nine months even on good days, but days spent doing nothing, challenged my emotional and physical capacities. Also, prior to my convalescence, my sister, Karen and I had planned a trip to Disney World, in Orlando Florida, with the kids. Karen had approached me about the idea about six weeks before when she found out about a business trip she needed to take there. She thought that it would be a perfect opportunity to engage the kids and have some fun. I had not flown on an airplane in six years, but I felt confident that I could do it. Of course, once I was placed on bed rest that changed the course of things. We decided to ask a dear friend of ours, who was presently helping me around the house everyday, Kathy Bell, if she would take my place. She enthusiastically accepted the position, and from there, the trip was back on. The night before the trip, I talked to each of the kids about their faith in God which they responded favorably to their relationship with him. Each of them agreed to say the prayer of salvation with me that night. With that in place, I was at peace letting them leave me for this fun filled trip that they had so been looking forward to since we originally told them about it. I knew that I couldn't control what happened to them on the trip, but I could reassure myself that if anything did happen to them, then we would all, one day, be reunited in heaven.

The kids were leaving early in the morning for their trip. That morning, my morning sickness was at its all time peak, leaving me hardly able to see the kids off. I knew then, as I suspected early on in the pregnancy, that whether I was on bed rest or not, the morning sickness would hold me back from many activities, especially traveling on an airplane to Disney World. It was one of those moments in life where you ask yourself, "Who am I kidding?" Morning sickness would rule my life during this pregnancy as it always had before. Well, the kids were off, and I planned to watch the news at noon for any incidents involving air travel during the morning rush. I figured no news was good news, and that's the way it was. However, the next day, the news reported a terrible incident involving a family vacationing in Orlando, who experienced a hotel invasion. The results of that traumatic event were not pretty. I thought to myself, "What are the chances of something bazaar, like that, happening while my family and friends are down there?" Of course, I called Karen and Kathy to make them aware of the situation, and make sure that they were on guard. They knew about it before I did, and they reassured me with their strategies for safety such as, everybody wearing the same t-shirts on the same day with a different color specified for each day. After that little scare, I just settled down and waited for the day to come when they would return.

On the Friday night before their return, Mark had to go out to attend the rehearsal practice and dinner for my brother, Carter's, wedding which was to take place the very next day. Mark was a groomsman in Carter and Elizabeth's wedding that coming Saturday. Friday was also my last day on the beloved, bed rest. Yeah, I had finally made it! I probably could have gone to the rehearsal also, but I still wasn't feeling that great. Also, everybody in my family kept talking to me about all the many stairs I would have to climb up in this building where the restaurant was located. Another thing, the restaurant was all the way up in Buckhead, so it wasn't close to home. Those two combinations didn't make the venture appeasing to me. I was perplexed by the description of the stair obstacle that everyone presented as such a problem. In my mind, I envisioned this huge gateway of stairs leading the way to the royal throne, and only the strongest could reach the top! During this time of the pregnancy, where I felt everything was out to get me, the simple things in life appeared as an ominous challenge. It would be six years later before I ever set foot into the infamous restaurant, Maggiano's, to behold the once, formidable stairway.

Since I was staying at home that night, Kathy Bell had instructed her two, teenage boys to come over and have dinner with me in order to keep me company. I owed them a dinner for all the help they had given us over the past few arduous months, so we set the date for that Friday night. It was a spectacular case of the blind leading the blind! Scott, the younger of the two, poured a large amount of lighter fluid on the charcoal and, in so doing, created an enormous fire for cooking the steaks. I don't remember how the steaks turned out, but I do remember supping on the delicious macaroni and cheese that Scott successfully concocted with all his infamous wizardry.  When dinner was over, the boys, politely, helped clean the kitchen and headed out to enjoy their Friday evening.  They had done their good deed for the day by tending to a sickly, older woman who was confined to house arrest.  I felt like I was one hundred and four years old.  All I was missing was my house coat and slippers!

Well, my big day had finally arrived!  I was freed from my bondage, and ready to recapture the life I wanted to live.  I got up that morning and decided to put on a Frank Sinatra rendition of "Our Wedding Day" in honor of my brother's wedding.  It was a beautiful day and perfect for a wedding!  We were first going to the airport to pick up the kids, and then we were headed to the wedding.  This was going to be a big day for me, since I hadn't been out of the house in two weeks.  When you're confined for any amount of time, you acclimate to your little world and anything outside of that world seems overwhelming.  And it was.  Just simply traveling on the expressway would take some adjustment due to the fast pace of the outside world and the vastness of the expansive roadways.  I was pleasantly surprised at how well I seemed to be adapting to all the outside stimuli.  It's amazing how quickly a person can get back into the flow of the world and all its demands after an extended convalescence.

We reached the airport and walked to our meeting place to meet the girls.

They found us first and came running and screaming with joy as they saw us approaching. They were thrilled with excitement at seeing us again and at sharing their experiences of their trip. We were engulfed with all their enthusiasm, and eager to hear all they had to say. Karen and Kathy seemed to be holding up well and appeared happy to have accomplished such a successful endeavor. We parted ways with the two chaperones and drove off to the wedding. We had some time on our hands, so Mark took us to the Buckhead Diner where we could all eat breakfast and catch up on all the latest events. I pushed myself to fight the nausea which had begun its tap dance in my stomach, and I planned on a strategy to keep me going during the wedding. I decided that I would take my muffin with me to the church and use it as back up in case I encountered a problem. During breakfast, Jordan began to complain about her stomach not feeling well. We just brushed it off as post-flying sickness, and pursued on with our engaging conversation. With muffin in hand and the assumption that Jordan would soon feel better, we left the diner and proceeded to the church. We got there a little early which gave us time to visit with family that we hadn't seen since I went out on bed rest. It was fun getting back into the game of life even though I was still felt somewhat handicapped in my current state. We sat down for the wedding to start, and Jordan wasn't getting any better. I also started feeling nauseated, so I started sneaking bits of my muffin into my mouth to keep the nausea at bay. As the bride walked down the aisle, I was sitting there eating and spilling crumbs on the church floor while also keeping my eyes on Jordan. I kept trying to encourage her that she would be fine. It finally came to a point where I felt that it was time for me to quietly sneak Jordan out and go to the nearest restroom. The minute we reached the first bathroom stall, Jordan "lost all her cookies!" Unbelievably, she was throwing up, and I was standing over her eating my muffin! How's that for motherhood 101? At first, we hoped against hope that she didn't have the dreaded stomach virus, so we shrugged it off as a one time incident. Of course, with the luck that we'd been having, the odds were against us. We said our good byes to everyone as we skipped the reception and drove home.

As luck would have it, Jordan did have the stomach virus, and that usually means that the rest of the family is susceptible to it also. In line with all of our other obstacles, this one would be no different. I was next in line to get the flu. I tolerated the throw up spells well, but I ran into complications with the oncoming fever that was beginning to have its way. I called the nurse at Dr. Schilling's office to ask her what I should do in case the fever got out of hand during the night. I was way too keenly aware of what a fever can do to a fetus, since Jamie struggled so much after the fever I had with her. I was definitely taking Tylenol to keep the fever down, but I didn't want to face a problem during the night, and then have to call the emergency room to ask for help. But that happened anyway! Even though

I had taken the Tylenol, my fever kept going higher during the middle of the night. My temperature was getting near 104 degrees and climbing. I finally broke down and called the hospital. The nurse just said that I would need to come in, so, I thought about getting Mark up to take me, but I heard him upstairs throwing up! Well, that option was out, so I called my sister, Karen. I'm always amazed at the ability Karen has to miss out on some of life's most opportune moments. As a footnote, one time Karen called everybody in the family to inform us all that our great aunt, Agnes, had died. Then she called back twenty minutes later to tell everybody that Agnes hadn't died yet! So, it didn't completely surprise me when she didn't answer the phone at two o'clock in the morning, after I called her about six times. Okay, so now what do I do? Well, I figured it was time to pray about it, and the answer came to me in a serene manner and with the purity of one of God's most precious commodities . . . water. I simply needed to drink a glass of water. I couldn't believe the instant effect that began to transpire. Gradually, but progressively, the fever started coming down. Over the next thirty minutes, I could incrementally feel my temperature cooling off. I was relieved, elated, thankful and bewildered that one of our most basic nutrients could have such a profound effect. With that peace of mind, I finally fell asleep.

The next morning, I awoke to a loud, grinding noise outside my window. I looked to see what was causing the noise, and it was the Henry County Water

Authority repairing a leak that had erupted in our front yard. It was fitting in light of the current events that had befallen us of late. The old saying, "If it can go wrong, it will," seemed to be our family's new anthem. However problematic the leak was, it didn't interfere with the healing process of the family to recover from the flu. I was happy to see Mark feeling so much better as the day ensued. He kept saying, "It feels so good to feel good!" The only problem that I had with that saying was that, thankfully, he was feeling better; however I was only marginally better. I was over the flu, but I wasn't over the pregnancy nausea. It was like Mark could take the "right of passage" into feeling well again, but I couldn't. That was okay with me because I knew that I was tougher then him anyway. I prided myself on my ability to handle uncomfortable, physical sickness since we women seem to get our fair share of it. I'd rather it be me than him tolerating the misery. At least one of us could feel good again. Everyone in the family eventually came down with the stomach flu, and everyone recovered just fine. I was glad that it was over, and relieved that we all had immunity to the virus for at least a year, typically speaking. The next step was to prepare for Jackie's ninth birthday!

After the stomach flu was over, things seemed to go smoothly for a while. We felt that all our bad luck was behind us, and we could move forward in a positive light. One day, during the afternoon, when the kids were home playing, I laid down on the sofa to take a rest. After a short while, I noticed a stomach cramp, down low in my abdomen, start to hurt. I tried to keep laying there in hopes that it would soon fade away, but it didn't, and I had to force myself up in order to alleviate the pain. I was annoyed at the problem, but I chose to ignore it. I went into the kitchen and prepared dinner. Although I still didn't feel my best, this was a precious time for me as I enjoyed making dinner and watching the kids play with their friends next door. Spring was in the air, I was at home with the kids, and life was mostly back in order. I love being in charge of my household. There's nothing more satisfying, for a mother, than running her house and caring for her family. It's one of life's best kept secrets.

Later that night, Mark and I laid down for a blissful night's sleep. At about two in the morning, I had another painful, lower abdominal cramp begin to surface. I found that the quicker that I got up out of the bed, the faster I could get control over the intensifying pain. I looked ridiculous getting out of the bed since I had to keep my body mostly straight until I reached a standing position. If I bent forward, the usually way of getting out of bed, then the cramp would intensify. I looked somewhat like a beached whale trying to get back into the ocean! I stayed up for a while to walk the cramp out. This was new to me, so I just guessed my best on how to treat it. Since I was familiar with muscle cramps, of all kinds from my gymnastics day, I took on the old athletic approach to work these cramps out. I was listening to my body and estimating the best way to correct the problem. It took me about an hour to work out the cramp as I paced the floor in the den, continually for an hour. After that, I was able to go back to bed and sleep. I told Mark about it the next day, and he, too, was puzzled about its cause. From this day forward, I began to experience these cramps on a regular basis, and now, I found myself on the threshold of a whole new phenomenon that I had never experienced before, and one that would challenge and incapacitate me as much as the depression had in the past.

I scheduled an appointment to see one of the doctors in Dr. Schilling's practice to discuss these symptoms and to hopefully find the solution. I met with Dr. Debra Haynes, and she performed a routine physical on me and evaluated my condition to determine the cause of the cramps. Her diagnosis was one of two possible causes. The first one, and the simplest to treat, was a low sodium balance in my body. The treatment was to just drink electrolyte based drinks such as Gatorade or Power Ade, etcetera. The other possibility, and the least appealing one, was that these cramps were caused by scar tissue build up around my abdominal muscles from the previous three c-sections that I had. Dr. Haynes instructed me to try the sodium based drinks first, and if I saw improvement, then we would know the cause and, we would have our solution. It's amazing how I can get so desperate over a situation that I go into over drive trying to correct the problem. Not only did I drink the Gatorade and other similar drinks, but I even went so far as to drink sodium, saturated Tomato juice! I thought to myself, "This is absurd, most pregnant women are warned to stay away from sodium, and here I was pouring it into my body with the force of Niagara Falls! At first, I thought that I did notice some improvement, but that hope was quickly vanished as the cramps kicked back in and took charge again. As was typical with the way this pregnancy was going, I was left to face the worst odds. It was now up to me to deal with this predicament. Once Dr. Haynes knew the case of my complaint, then the best she could do was to advise me that these cramps would get worse before they got better due to the inevitable increasing size of the uterus over the next five months. It was explained to Mark and me that the scar tissue was attached to the uterus, and as the uterus grew, the scar tissue would continue to tug on the abdominal muscles. This condition would last the entire pregnancy! So, I was back in that old familiar corner of life, where the odds continue to beat me down until I've got nothing to hold onto, except my faith. As great as my faith was, sometimes it seemed not to be enough. I had already faced many, insurmountable odds in the beginning of this pregnancy, and now, I was beginning to lose my strength. I left the doctor's office feeling defeated . . . again.

I tried to persevere as I dealt with my new predicament. I ran with my usual routine of the day, often stopping to rest my belly. Dispersed throughout the day, the cramps would surface, and I would spend a considerable amount of time walking them out. The nausea and constant flu-like feeling accompanied me everyday along with a consistent, but light, tugging through around my abdomen. I simply put one foot in front of the other, and tried my best to overcome this ill fate. I also, continued to feel overly paranoid about many things such as, choking while eating, food allergies, food poisoning and other evils that could occur at anytime. One of the reasons that I was so fearful had to do with the fact that I was only on one psychiatric medicine that was helping me stay afloat, but it wasn't comprehensive enough to cover all my inadequacies. The other reason for the relentless fear was that physically, I didn't feel good. I have found that whenever I'm sick, it's hard to think positive thoughts. It's easy to feel that something is constantly out to get you. When I feel good, then I believe that I can conquer the world. These combined fears only complicated matters for me. I was living in agony, most of the time, due to all of the aliments that I was battling everyday.

As day turned into night, the cramps became relentless to the point that I would find myself pacing the den floor for one or two hours at a time. I tried to find some fun while enduring the experience by looking out the windows to see what was going on in the neighborhood at night. One time, I remembered seeing a neighbor's bathroom light on which usually wasn't, and I thought, *wonder what's up with them?* Misery loves company, so I tried to find any association to keep me company, and I was easily amused. I also used the hours, spent pacing the floor at night, to work things out in my head that needed my attention such as figuring out a way to ensure my kids safety while they visited some dear friends that had moved to Lake Oconee. I was dreadfully fearful of them having an accident involving the lake even though we knew they were in good hands with the parents of the friends they were visiting. Another fear that I would contemplate in my head during the "wee" hours of the mornings was that of a stray cat that had appeared in our back yard. I was raised to believe that any stray animal was accompanied with rabies! This little cat had been visiting for about a week, and I had tolerated my fears well, but in the middle of the night, everything in my imagination could easily get blown out of proportion. After a night spent walking and figuring things out, I called my sister, Karen, the next day, and I asked her if she would take the cat to the vet for its shots. She obliged me, and I felt much better afterward. Now, I could move on and focus on the next issue to resolve at night during my routine walk.

It quickly became apparent to me that trying to sleep in my bed at night was no longer an option. No matter what position I laid in, I would get a cramp. Actually, within seconds of lying down, a cramp would force its way up screaming at me with tightness and pain. That was it; I was headed for the recliner in the den for the duration of the pregnancy. I use the word, recliner, relatively speaking because I could only recline the chair a few inches. I mostly sat up straight in the chair with an occasional opportunity to push the chair back a few inches. Now that I could find a position to sleep in, the next obstacle was to overcome the lack of sleep itself. Even through the recliner was more beneficial for me; I could still awaken to the pain of a cramp. Actually, at first, all the recliner did for me was to allow me faster access to get to my feet once a cramp came on. One night, I was so bothered by the cramps, that I didn't fall asleep until five o'clock in the morning. Even though it was summer time, and the kids were out of school, they would get up early in the morning to watch cartoons. On this particular morning, Mark and the kids were up at seven o'clock in the morning, and I'd had a total of two hours of sleep! Needless to say, I was beside myself that morning. I lost all control, and Mark called the doctor's office to get me in that day to further discuss the problem and see if anything could be done. Mark's secretary, Jackie Moddle, took me to the doctor's office for my appointment. All I can say is thank God for his angels! I saw one of the mid-wives that day who provided me with the ammunition I needed to fight back. She miraculously had all the answers! I told her that I couldn't go on living this way, and she taught me how to win back my life. The first and most helpful remedy she provided for me was Tylenol PM to take every night at bedtime. The next piece of advice she gave me was to go buy one of those beautiful, pregnancy girdles. She said that it would give me more support for the uterus and subsequently relieve some of the triggering of the cramps. The third piece of the puzzle, that would bring all my troubles to halt, was that I needed to take vitamin B-6 also known as, Nextrex. This would curb the relentless nausea, and subdue the acid that kept me from enjoying food. Upon absorbing all of this new information, I felt as if a huge burden had been lifted from my shoulders. I felt much better knowing that there were things that I could do to combat these series of events. I left the office with a renewed sense of confidence that I could just possibly make it through this pregnancy after all. From that moment on, many of my problems subsided, and I indulged in the relief, but I wasn't completely free from all the complexities of this pregnancy.

It was hard to believe that these three, simple, yet, key remedies could have such a profound effect. I was now in a much better position to handle the ongoing cramps and any other obstacles that threatened my existence along this path. The Tylenol PM worked like a charm! The first time I took it, I remembered watching Jay Leno, on his show, while I waited for the inducement of sleep to occur. It was the most welcomed feeling in the world to feel, for the first time in months, drowsiness engulf me into a peaceful, blissful sleep. There was a God! I awoke the next morning feeling like a new person. I remember telling Mark that as long as I could sleep like that every night, then I could handle the cramps and anything else that came along. I was beginning to feel like I was superwoman, and that I could take on anything. The old saying, "An ounce of prevention is worth a pound of cure, rang volumes in my ears that day." But the show wasn't over yet. Things were tremendously better, but I still had four months to go before my due date. I still continued to sleep in the recliner which would be my bed for the rest of the pregnancy. That was fine with me as long as I could sleep, which I was able to do. As the weeks progressed, so did the intensity and duration of the cramps. I began to give in to the strong hold that the cramps dictated on a daily basis. They came during the day and at night. They had a mind of their own, and they would come on me without notice. I had no control over them, but they had control over me. After a while, I was afraid to leave the house. I was right back where I had been so many years ago with the depression and anxiety that prevented me from leaving the house. Once again, I was encapsulated by fear and anguish leaving me hopeless and weak. Since the cramps could spring up at any moment, without the slightest hint of the oncoming onslaught, then I feared being in public under the duress of an attack. First of all, I didn't want people to see me in that predicament. It was inexplicable to others that were not familiar with my plight, and somewhat embarrassing to reveal in public. Secondly, with the intensity and durability of these cramps, I was frightened by the fact that they could possibly rupture my uterus and put me into a real emergency. I had once dreaded being confined to the house when I was on bed rest, and this wasn't much different. Other than performing my regular household chores, it was difficult to find ways to stay occupied and pass the time. I was beginning to sink back into the "days of old" with my self deprecating attitude. I was allowing my physical limitations to control my life. The doctor hadn't placed limitations on me this time, but I had.

## Chapter Six

### A Faith Filled Discovery

The breaking point came one morning after I had an unusual, restless night with two cramps that were set off throughout the night. Once again, I had very little sleep, and I awoke early to the sounds of the kids getting up. Mark joyfully marched through the den, where I was sleeping, and recited his great plans for his day. I was so dismayed that I had no plans for the day other than to sulk and suffocate in my misery. I followed Mark into the bathroom trying to explain how awful I felt. I cried like a baby and complained until Mark had enough. He snapped back at me and called me a baby! He told me to quit crying and to get over it! Not only did his words shock and surprise me, but thankfully, they incited me to fight back! I now realized that I had fallen to bottom of the pit, and I now realized that I had two choices. One choice was to continue on the downward spiral path complaining all the time or I was going to pull myself up by my "boot straps" and do something about my situation. Since I was already at the lowest depth that I could ever imagine being in, then I knew that I only, really had one choice. I had to come out swinging. When you're at the bottom, there is only one place to go, and that place is up. And that's where I set my mind to go. At this point, I realized that it was do or die. Mark's scolding remarks prompted me into the turning point that would pull me out of the viper's pit that I had placed myself in. You never tell any of the Cantrell's that we can't do something. You never challenge a Cantrell to a duel, unless you expect a good fight. With that I moved forward with renewed strength and vitality. It wasn't an instant recovery, but it was the beginning of a great discovery process. Later that day, I finally went out to lunch with the family to our local Pharmacy, Eagle's Landing Pharmacy, which had the old fashioned soda fountain. My appetite wasn't very good, but I managed to choke down a grilled cheese sandwich. Whether or not I enjoyed my meal was of no consequence, but the fact that I was out of the house was monumental. As the ensuing days followed along, I tried to continue with the same effort to get on with my life. It wasn't always easy, but I kept trying. I was relying on my own courage and strength to motivate myself forward. What I didn't realize was that I had taken on all the responsibility without including my chaperone in life . . . God. I figured that I had exuded good faith all my life, and I thought that my faith was strong at this current time. I soon learned that when God wants you to "step it up, he'll allow you to go as far as you can on your own, until he gets your attention long enough for you to listen to his message. One night, some friends of ours, Mike Pickett and his girlfriend, Nancy, came to visit and to show us a video of an Evangelist, by the name of David Ring, who they had recently met. Mike and Nancy are not "holy rollers" who go around hitting people over the head with the Bible. They are simple Christians who recognize a credible story when they see it. The title of the video was *why do Bad Things Happen to Good People?* I didn't want to watch the video because that's exactly how I felt. I felt that bad things were constantly happening to me, and I was afraid that more bad things would come. I didn't want to hear a sermon on how I should act. I was already feeling bad enough about the way things were, and I didn't need preaching to straighten me out. I already knew about faith. I had more faith than most people do, so why did I have to improve? I didn't need to do better for God; he needed to do more for me. He needed to swoop down and save me from all my pain and agony. Well that attitude was about to change!

I didn't have any other choice but to watch the David Ring video. This evangelist happens to have Cerebral Palsy. I thought to myself, that I would almost rather have Cerebral Palsy than to suffer what I was going through. There was nothing specific about what David Ring said that hit me over the head, but somewhere along the line, his message got through to me. The overall message was that, with God all things are possible. Even though I already knew this, seeing the scripture in action was quite convincing. One of his greatest lines was, "I have Cerebral Palsy; what's your problem? I thought, "Well, presently my problem is cramps, but after hearing his story, mine didn't seem so bad. I couldn't believe I was actually thinking this way. For months, I had allowed myself to be the victim, and I believed that nobody was going through anything as challenging as me. But here was this man saying, that my challenge is no different than another person's challenge. My problem was not the physical aspect of my pregnancy, but the way I was handling my situation. I was relying entirely on myself and my own strength to get through this ordeal. David Ring's message was simple; rely on God. With that message ingrained in me, I began, for the first time in months, to move forward with a renewed outlook on life. I was beginning to let go and let God. As I unleashed the burden of my pain and fear on him, I was able to take on a whole new approach to life. I started relying on God for my every endeavor. I trusted in God, implicitly to get me through everything life had to offer. The very next day, I started off in good spirits I had a renewed faith that was unquenchable! I took all my concerns to him in prayer, and I knew, without a doubt, that he was walking alongside me. Now, I was literally walking in faith. From this point onward, I would see the world in a whole new light. What a revelation! One of the first changes that I noticed in myself was that I was becoming less fearful about everything that had previously clogged my mind. Anytime a fear came up, I would just pray about it, and every time I prayed, I would hear that still, small voice telling me that everything would be fine. With that in mind, I started going out into the world again! I would go to the grocery store. If a cramp started, and they always did, I would just relax my mind and continue to shop. I would think to myself, "What's the difference in walking out a cramp here or eat home?" The real fear was, "What if a cramp gets too bad for me to handle?" I'll be a freak show in front of other people! People will stare at me in horror! Nobody will know what to do with me! Another question that came to mind was, "What if I get into real trouble and the uterus ruptures?" The answer to all of this was . . . God is in control, and I can do this. It's one thing to "talk the talk"; it's a whole other adventure to actually, "walk the walk". I designed a plan, everywhere I went, of how to handle my cramps while out in public. I strategically located every bathroom and every place that I would feel comfortable walking out my cramps without anybody noticing. It was great! I was out of the house, and I was happening! Concerns over my uterus rupturing or any other unforeseeable prospective tribulations vanished from my head as I plunged forward into my new found faith.

Just about the time I was beginning life anew, I had an interesting occurrence one morning while Mark and the kids were at church. I stayed home from church that day for happy reasons. The kids were starting school the next day, and I couldn't wait to pack their little school bags! As miniscule as this seems, it was a treat for me. I was in great spirits, and then a cramp came on me that persevered with a vengeance. I kept up my good spirits as I reassured myself that this, too, would pass. And then it didn't. I continued to walk and pray for the cramp to subside, but it wouldn't. I started to perspire and feel nausea from the pain. I started thinking of people that I knew close by that could come help me if things progressively got worse. The grinding pain pierced my abdomen like nothing I had ever felt before. I was beginning to wonder if this was the beginning of a rupture. I held on, and called the doctor's office. Pam Garrett, Dr. Schilling's Physician's Assistant, returned my call and reassured me that it was not very probable for the uterus to rupture. The way she said it, gave me the peace that I needed. Eventually, the pain and the cramp started to loose their hold on me.

After Mark and the kids got home, I explained what happened to him, and he seemed surprised at the level of pain that this cramp had elicited. I comforted him with the words that Pam had spoken to me, and with that he was at ease. Plus, I had a new lease on life. I could handle anything! Later on that day, I did endure another cramp that would rock the rector scale that measures earthquakes, but it didn't last as long.

The next day, I did see Dr. Schilling at my scheduled appointment time. When I inquired about the previous day's events, I asked him if my uterus could rupture. His crazy response was, "We haven't lost one yet!" I wanted to ask him, "Was that the same response your physician gave you when you had your vasectomy?" Of course, that was Dr. Schilling's way of letting me know that I had nothing to worry about. Amazingly enough that was the last of the severe cramps that caused me the intense pain. All cramps were painful, but I knew they weren't life threatening like those two, previous ones had appeared to be. Regular cramps were mostly an annoyance because they were long lasting. I didn't know at the time, that I would never suffer another radical cramp, but with my new found faith, I didn't worry about it either. With all my fears conquered, I pressed on with a smile on my face and with confidence in my heart. What freedom! I grew to love God more everyday; not because he was doing what I wanted, but because of what he was showing me. This new faith that I was discovering, tremendously impacted my life! I could have never handled any of this by myself. It was all God. He didn't just say, "Here, I'll take away those cramps." He said, "Lean on me, and I'll get you through it." His message rang loud and clear, "Have faith in me, and together, you and I can handle it." And he kept his promise to me. No matter where I went or what I did, I had confidence that he was with me. While I was busy relishing in my new found, faith and my new freedom, I contemplated upon my creation. It occurred to me, that even though I had been born with the genetic trait of OCD, which predisposed me to severe postpartum depression and titled me as A-Typical Bipolar, that God doesn't make junk! I've always blamed myself for being weak and for my imperfections, and now I realized that God made me in his image. If I'm good enough for God, then I'm good enough! What another great revelation! I've heard these things all my life, but when I applied them to my disability, I gained a whole new perspective of myself.

As the next couple of months went by I continued to walk strongly in my new faith. I started going to the movies with my sister Karen, and friend Kathy Bell, along with the kids. I ventured out shopping and even picked out new canisters for my kitchen. I was on a roll. Mark and I would go out and furniture shop. I did all this with the faith of a saint and the courage of a lion. And that's what it took. While I was out on these ventures, I would encounter cramps, and I would find a place to walk them out. I never let on to others what was going on inside me. I just kept on going! I particularly remember one morning that I was scheduled for an ultra sound at Dr. Schilling's office with the technician, Mary. I was all dressed up and ready to go when I was stopped in my tracks by a cramp. I couldn't drive the car under this influence because I needed to stand erected. I walked and prayed that I wouldn't be late to my appointment because the wrath of Mary might be worse than the wrath of God! I knew that I would make it to my appointment on time, and I did. "If ye ask, then ye shall receive." Everything seemed to be falling into place just beautifully. As long as I made the effort, I could do anything I wanted to do. Now that we were getting closer to the big day, my friends were throwing me showers left and right. Everyone and everything in life was back to normal and happy. The confidence in the kids started to come back, and I could see it in their faces. Jamie, especially, had a hard time when I wasn't feeling well. She would internalize my stomach aches, and she caused her stomach to hurt to the point that she wouldn't eat. I took her to a Gastroenterologist to have her checked because she had actually lost weight. Nothing scared me more than seeing her that skinny. Once I quit complaining about my stomach pains, her belly aches also went away. She was now doing much better. Other obstacles that we had overcome during the pregnancy were that of me being exposed to Fifth's disease *three* times! From what I've been told, Fifth's disease got it's name because it was the fifth disease in the family of diseases that were so prevalent in the late 1800's and early 1900's such as Mumps, Measles, Rubella, and Chicken Pox. Fifth's disease is only harmful to a pregnant woman during the first trimester and only if she hasn't been exposed to it before pregnancy. Most people have been exposed to it, and it usually doesn't create a problem. However, with the knowledge that I had been exposed to it, meant that I had to get tested. Dr. Schilling explained that the worst thing that could happen if I did catch the illness and did pass it on to the baby would be that I would have to undergo an intrauterine blood transfusion! No problem! I just laughed as I told him, "That's easy compared to everything else that I've been through!" I also got tested for Gestational Diabetes twice. The first time, I had to repeat the test, but I eventually passed. One month before I was due, the nurse called and said that I needed to be tested again. I thought, "Does it really matter this late in the game?" My results placed me at borderline diabetic, but once again, I passed! Now all we had to do was wait for the big day and the new arrival! We were on the home stretch and I was running the bases!

During the whole pregnancy, I had one focus . . . when is delivery? The possible dates for the delivery vacillated between the middle and the latter part of my grueling nine months. My original due date was November 5, 1998, but with a scheduled c-section, I was hoping for a two week early intervention. That's the way Dr. Schilling usually did things, but, apparently Dr. Schilling wanted to jolt me around. The whole last month of the pregnancy I saw him weekly, and I tried at each visit to pin him down with a date. At one point, he actually talked of moving the date forward by two weeks putting me within two days of my original due date! I thought to myself, "What's this?" My heart sank into my stomach as I waited with baited breath for his final response. He finally chose October 26, 1998! Hooray! We had a date that was about ten day's earlier than my original date, and that was good enough for me! I felt like I was getting ready to reach my final exams in collage. I had a date! I was so excited! I sat down with Stacey, the scheduler, to arrange the details. On my next scheduled appointment, which was a week later, I would also go to the hospital and have my pre-op work done. We were finally coming to the end of this long and arduous ordeal! The wheels were in motion, and I feel like graduation day was upon us. It's pitiful that the most exciting day in a pregnant woman's life is the day of her doctor's appointment, but that's the life of a pregnant woman. Every visit is an exciting insight to the growth of the baby and a step forward to the big day. Now, things were finally going my way, and life was getting exciting. Preparation for the birth was now in progress.

It was all systems go!

During the last week before delivery, we all went through the usual motions of getting everything pulled together for the delivery. The girls were all excited and restless as they helped me get things done. All the baby sitters and clean-up crews' made their final plans. The week went smoothly, and I didn't get stressed out about the last minute details as I usually did in the past. Finally October twenty-third came which was my last doctor's appointment, and it was followed by my pre-op work at the hospital. Kathy Bell went with me because two heads are better than one, especially when it comes to Kathy and me. After my final appointment with Dr. Schilling, I said my good byes to all the staff at the office and headed over to the hospital for the pre-op. It was a beautiful Friday, and the air around us was filled with happiness and anticipation. Of course, it was also the weekend, so most people were in a good mood whether I was having a baby or not! When Kathy and I reached the hospital, I couldn't believe all the changes that had been made over the past six years. The maternity ward now had its own surgery room and recovery room as well as all the regular maternity rooms. For the first time, I would not have to be transferred from floor to floor between surgery, recovery and the maternity floor. Everything would take place in the same area on the same floor. Kathy also noticed another change. She observed the other ages of the mother's that had signed in before me, and at age thirty-six, I was the oldest one there. In fact, looking at the ages of the other expecting moms, I was almost a Grandmother. We had a big laugh at that one. Once I was seated in a room for my interview, different nurses would come in and take their turn doing the ritualistic process of questions and pokes and prods that I new all too well. I stumped one nurse when I explained my delicate situation about the cramps. She looked star struck at me as she asked me how I slept at night. When I told her that I slept in a recliner for the last five months of the pregnancy, she looked slightly amazed! While talking with this nurse, I also could voice my concerns about the anesthesia and possible complications involving the cramps. Not only did I get a chance to vent all of my fears and concerns, but I actually got to talk to the anesthesiologist that day! We went over everything about my past, present and future, and before it was over, I was greatly relieved at all he had to say. I came away from the pre-op confident, relaxed, happy and sporting a new fashion . . . hospital identification bracelets! I had at least four! They would go great with my outfit that I had planned to wear that night to our last, public function that we would attend for a while. We were to attend the Charity Ball Gala at Eagle's Landing Country Club that Friday night. It was the hit party of the year and everybody who was anybody would be there! Not really; it was just a packed house with a lot of fun people! We were looking forward to it; however, I was so caught up with excitement and busy packing and last minute arrangements that I wore myself out. We had to stay home, but we were just as happy in doing so. Mark was somewhat relieved that we stayed home because he really felt that we needed to rest up and gear up for the big event that following Monday. All the kids were out that night having their own fun with different friends and functions, so we had a nice, peaceful night all to ourselves. We were completely caught off guard when the doorbell rang at eleven o'clock that night. Apparently, my sister, Karen, decided that if we couldn't go to the party, then the party would come to us! And so it did. All of a sudden our house was filled to capacity with friends and well wishers who came to celebrate with us! We were aghast at the homage our friends had chosen to pay us that night. We had a blast, and there are pictures to prove it! Unbelievably, we stayed up until one o'clock in the morning until the last partiers left. I must have really been having a good time to stay up that late! Everybody eventually went home, and we retired to bed with happy thoughts bouncing in our heads!

The next day, Saturday, I spent preparing my birthing announcements, so they would be ready to go as soon as we had a picture of the new baby with her sisters. I had all the envelopes addressed and stamped and ready to go. The kids joined in and loved helping out. The next day, Sunday, was business as usual, and I stayed home while Mark and the kids went to church. I did my own Bible study by pulling out the Bible and watching a preacher on television give his sermon. It was unbelievable how pertinent that his message was for me. It was titled, *be Anxious for Nothing.* The sermon went, "Be anxious for nothing, but in all things pray with thanksgiving in your heart and confess your needs to the Lord for he will answer your prayer." That one verse was all I needed to hear. As I went through the Bible Study, that particular verse became ever more compelling. The message from the Bible was ingrained in me to the point that I no longer had any doubt in my mind or my heart that the surgery and delivery would go well. I had feared the surgery during the entire pregnancy because I was all too familiar with possible complications that could happen, and I had my mental condition to consider. Possible depression, anxiety, complications from the surgery, and abdominal cramps were just a few of the concerns that I had, but that was all gone with one simple Bible verse, "Be anxious for nothing." Mark and the girls came home from church, and we enjoyed having lunch together as a family. Later that day, the girls would head off to Kathy Bell's house to stay over the next few days.

Shortly after lunch, I began to notice that I was having a lot of "trigger happy" cramps. They didn't last that long, but they kept on coming. About four o'clock that afternoon, when Karen and Kathy came to pick up the kids, I told Karen about the cramps, and she was worried for me. I laughed as I said, "Karen, these are the last of the cramps; after tomorrow, I'll never have another cramp again!" With that, she was happy. Mark and I kissed the kids good bye, which was bittersweet under these conditions, but nonetheless, a good send off. Mark and I retreated back into the house and waited for Mike and Nancy to come over for dinner. They insisted on bringing us dinner that night, and since Mike owned several restaurants called, *Buffalo's Cafe*, then we couldn't turn down good food like that. I had continued to undergo constant cramping to the point that I realized that I was having contractions. At first, I was afraid to eat dinner because I didn't want to go into full labor during the night with a full stomach. Nancy encouraged me to eat, and the minute I soaked my teeth into that luscious hamburger, my contractions stopped. That's the way it always happens. You can never out smart Mother Nature! Mike and Nancy were a tremendous positive influence on us that night as we talked and laughed about everyday events in life, instead of focusing on our apprehensions about the next day's delivery. Mike is never one to stay out late, which is one thing I like about him, so they left at nine thirty in the evening. Mark and I were both pleasantly sleepy and ready for bed. Instead of being nervous and anxious like we had in the past, we were blessed by the presence of angels, who came in the form of Mike and Nancy, and left us in perfect peace. Mark headed off to the bedroom, and I retreated to my chair! I had become very acquainted with my new friend, my chair. I turned on the television and found that the movie *Pretty Woman* was on, and I decided to watch it. Julia Roberts and Richard Gere kept me entertained until I drifted off to sleep. The only thing that kept me awake on this night was the baby tap dancing on my bladder! I drank a lot of water that night before I went to sleep, so that I wouldn't be thirsty in the morning. Between the frequent trips to the bathroom and the tap dancing kid, I was up some during the night, but at least I wasn't walking out a cramp.

The big day was finally here and not a moment too soon! This was the day we had all been waiting for . . . Jenae's debut and my liberation! That may not be the nicest way of thinking about your child's birth, but that was the reality of the situation. The alarm buzzed at four o'clock in the morning, and I awoke easily to its blaring sound. Okay . . . here we go . . . it's time to put the plan into action as rehearsed in our heads a million times. I took a deep breath and put one foot in front of the other while persuading myself to keep the faith. My thoughts rippled through a tide of thoughts that motivated me through the morning preparations. Convincing thoughts that I uttered to myself were, "Don't look back, and don't think about needing more time to prepare for this." The statement that McCauley Caulkin made in the movie, *Home Alone,* "Okay, don't get scared now," was my anthem for the morning's prep work. Somehow, I managed to stay focused in present time, and I never did look back wishing for more time to psychologically prepare for this day. I got dressed and put on my makeup like this was an average day. The last thing I put in my suitcase was my Bible and my Bible Study book. I took my rings off and placed my cross in the change purse of my wallet. Mark and I grabbed our coats and off we went. I looked at my neighbor, Jenny Stephen's house, as we pulled out of the driveway and wondered if anybody was watching and saying, "There they go." Jenny had been such an encouraging source of strength for my family and me during all the difficult times, and she motivated me to stay strong and never waver. Of course, I must have a huge ego to think that people are up at four o'clock in the morning to see us leave. Yes, everybody is camping out just to watch us leave for the hospital! Aside from that silly thought, we drove down the quite, street enjoying the peaceful moment that the pre-dawn atmosphere provided. Neither of us had much to say, but when we did speak, it was about simple, everyday type things that we needed to do at some point. We finally reached the hospital which was only a mile away. Thankfully, we didn't have a long drive which would have allowed us more time to obsess over the upcoming events and possible reactivate our previous jitters. Once we arrived at the hospital, we were calm and ready for action. I was impressed by the calmness that accompanied me as I opened the door to exit the car. The sense of peace that drenched my mind and soul at this time was incomprehensible to me. I had never allowed myself to experience this feeling before. I knew that God was walking with Mark and me and answering the prayers of many people who held us close in their prayers during the long and difficult months.

It's funny how I paid attention to all the little details of our entrance into the hospital. My senses were heightened and my eyes were observant to the simplest, most common place objects that comprised the decor of the hospital. Mark and I gave our greetings at the front desk and headed up to the maternity floor for our official check in. Once again, McCauley Caulkin's words rang in my head, "Okay, don't get scared now." Once we were in the maternity ward that was it. All apprehensions were left at the door, as the nurses immediately took charge and initiated the pre-op procedures. Obviously, the first step was to get me into that lovely *Victoria Secret* nightgown that sets the fashion world in a tizzy! Next step . . . the release of those supportive, yet unsightly maternity briefs! Never again would I be placed in a position where I would ever have to don a garment like that. Don't get me wrong, those beautiful briefs had been a friend of mine during my time of need, but the thrill in the removal of the elephant sized girdle, was the sense of freedom that would soon be mine. Barry White, the only person who can so eloquently write love songs about the removal of women's lingerie, couldn't even capture the moment of happiness I felt as I left those briefs behind! I shot out of the bathroom, dressing room, like a pro football player ready for the Super Bowl, and my staff was waiting for me. I eagerly climbed onto the bed, so the official, life support, *hook up,* could begin. Tubes, needles and antiseptics were all a part of my new accessory assortment. I was ready for all the apparatus to be attached, especially the catheter. Catheters are not usually thought about as a pleasant object of desire, but when you've been rushing to the bathroom every five minutes of the day, it brings a welcomed relief. Now that I was basically strapped to the bed, I hoped and prayed that a cramp wouldn't develop. If one began, then I wouldn't be able to get up and walk it out. I was hoping that I would get the epidural before I would have a cramp, so the numbing effect of the medicine could take care of the pain. I expressed my concerns to the nurse, and she looked at me like I had no option but to stay put. At one point, I did start to get a cramp, and I hoped it would stay at bay. Thankfully, it did keep quiet, and I didn't have to worry about it too much. One nurse came in and hooked up the baby heart monitor to my belly in order to get an accurate reading on the baby's heartbeat. She noticed that I was having contractions, and she stated that the baby didn't like the contractions. I thought, "Lady, if you're trying to scare me, you're nine months too late!" I had started having contractions at four months gestation, and they continued throughout the pregnancy. Now, here I am, five minutes from having a c-section, and she thinks this is something to worry about? I had the upper hand on the outcome of this situation!

My new anesthesiologist, Dr. Anita Tolentino, came in to meet me for the first time. By this time I already had the intra-venous solution pumping in my arm and my concentration was beginning to waver, but I made every effort to correctly pronounce Dr. Tolentino's last name. I thoroughly discussed with her all of my concerns about the delivery process, including my predisposition to anxiety, my previous encounter with a panic attack during my last surgery, and the potential for an abdominal cramp to spring forward without notice. Dr. Tolentino eased my fears as she explained all of my options, and we decided to hold off on any premature medications that would put me to sleep during the surgery. The plan was that she would administer a sedative at any time I felt that it was necessary. We felt confident that I could go into the surgery unaffected by drug-induced drowsiness, and that if a problem arose, then she would provide me with the necessary medication. I knew after meeting her for a few minutes, that she was a God-send.

Another visitor stopped by to see me that morning. She was the nurse that did all of my pre-op work. She and I struck up a good report on pre-op day, and she came by to wish me "good luck". I was overwhelmed at her act of kindness. She was such a sweetheart. That's one of the many reasons that I felt so confident in delivering at Henry Medical Center. With every delivery that I've had there, they have treated me like royalty. That tender loving care goes a long way when you are experiencing the most dramatic event in your life with the birth of a baby. There was another nurse that took good care of me that morning. She was on the night shift, so I was her patient during the early morning hours when I first arrived. She and I became engrossed in conversation about cats. She was a cat lover and expert, and I was a spastic new *cat* owner. She calmed my fears about having a cat and a baby. She had such a calm demeanor about her, that I was mesmerized by her insight into the animal world. In her few simple, reassuring words, she taught me a lot about cats and also about life. That's why it's always important for people to try to encourage each other with words of wisdom. You never know the lasting effect that it can have on another person.

It was getting later in the morning when my fan club finally arrived. That would include Mike Pickett and my sister Karen. They were both appointed to camera duty for the day's big event. This was a very important calling for these two, and Mark and I only hoped they would get it right. Putting Karen and Mike in charge of any responsibility is like giving two of *The Three Stooges* a job. You never quite know how things are going to turn out. And finally, the master of ceremonies, arrived . . . the one, the only . . . Dr. Schilling. It was now, officially, show time!

I didn't remember seeing Mark and Dr. Schilling leave, but all of a sudden the room was quiet, and someone was wheeling me out of the room and down the hall to the Operating Room (OR). McCauley Caulkin's statement ran through my mind again, "Okay, don't get scared now." We reached the doors to the OR, and they automatically opened up wide for me to enter. I glanced around the room quickly trying to access the atmosphere where I would spend some of the most crucial moments of my life. There was such vastness to the sterile, white room that

I could only absorb some of its character. I had never been in this OR before, so everything was completely new to me. I mostly remember the white, sterile feel it had. They rolled me over to the table where the surgery would be performed. I thought, "You expect me to lift my oversized body up, from this nice wide bed, and move myself to this tiny, narrow table that you call a bed?" And the answer was . . . yes! I retracted my thoughts back to my gymnastics days, and my life spent on the four inch balance beam. I thought that if I could perform on the balance beam, in front of hundreds of people, then I guess I could move my enormous belly from this comfortable, large bed onto that skinny piece of apparatus that they called a table. I was successful in my attempt as I made it on the first try. Quickly after I was situated on the table, Dr. Tolentino pricked my lower back to administer the spinal block which was totally different than what I had had in the past. Mostly every woman is familiar with the epidural which is commonly used for c-sections and regular deliveries as well, however, studies have shown that the spinal block is much more effective for this surgery and provides a faster recovery. I felt the slight sting of the needle, and that was it. They began to lay me down flat on the table! I had not laid flat on my back in seven months! I smiled in amazement as I slowly went back into a fully reclined position. The spinal block had already taken effect, so I had no worries! Another hurdle jumped, and now things were really beginning to roll.

I laid there perfectly calm and relaxed hoping that this feeling would last. It felt good to finally be able to give all my physical and mental concerns over to the experts, and to let them work their magic. I was comforted by arms that were stronger than mine. As things progressed, Mark was finally allowed access into the room. During the pregnancy, he questioned whether or not he could watch me undergo another surgery, but when the time finally arrived, he waltzed into the OR, wearing his doctor's uniform, with the confidence of warrior. He was actually more relaxed this time than he had ever been before. They positioned him right next to me and, closer than I remembered from the past surgeries. Apparently, he gets braver every time I have one of these surgeries, and this time he really surprised me and himself as he actually looked over at my belly during the surgery.

Position at the head of the table, was Dr. Tolentino, my guardian angel, carefully watching over me and monitoring my condition. She talked to me about all kinds of things to keep my mind off of the surgery. She and I got into a fun conversation about super models and other celebrities that were current in the new. We had a great time conversing and sharing opinions about Hollywood's great celebrities and others. We had most of the world's problems solved before the surgery was over.

And now, for the moment that we've all been waiting for . . . the arrival and first breathe of Jenae Marie Brittain! I felt the old familiar "tugging" on my abdomen which signified that Dr. Schilling was getting ready to pull the baby out. Tug one, tug two and here she was . . . Jenae Marie Brittain had made her debut! She let out this itty, bitty, scratchy little cry, and she was fine. I thought since her cry was so demure that she must be tiny, and she was. She weighed in at six pounds, thirteen ounces, and she was nineteen inches long. Jenae was actually one ounce heavier than Jordan was when she was born, but you couldn't tell it by looking at her. After they cleaned her up and wrapped her in a blanket, they brought her over to me. Of course, I couldn't hold her, but this was the first time they had ever placed a baby right next to my face! I was surprised by that gesture and by the size of the baby. I thought that she was the smallest baby that we had delivered, but she wasn't. Her little head was so petite, and she looked over at me with those beady, dark eyes as if to say, "What's all the commotion about?"

After our brief encounter, a nurse took her away to the nursery, but this time the hospital staff did something totally different. They placed Jenae in Mark's arms and escorted him to the nursery with Jenae in tow! Mark was almost in shock. As he and Jenae and the nurse exited the OR, Karen recorded great footage of him on the video camera looking down at Jenae and saying, "Karen, I can't believe how small this baby is!" After that, Karen continued taping great shots of Jenae getting her first bath and getting her footprints made. Once Karen captured the first moments of Jenae's life on camera, she briskly walked over to the pay phone to call my Mom and Dad and tell them the good news. We have proof of that phone call, because Karen left the camera running the entire time that she was rushing down the hall to the pay phone to make the call, and all you can see on the video is the hospital floor bouncing around. I said it before; she's a wiz with the camera! And not only was she doing her job well, but the other camera man, Mike Pickett, was also snapping away pictures of Jenae and Mark on their escort from the OR to the nursery. What Karen taped on video of Jenae, Mike got on snapshot. So the two cameramen/stooges came through for us after all.

Once I was wheeled out of the OR, the nurse stopped by the nursery so that I could see Jenae again. She was very healthy and also very mad that she was getting a bath and having work done on her. After that brief stop, I was moved into my maternity room for the duration of my stay. Mark and I were already reveling in delight at the smooth order of events during the entire morning. The surgery was flawless, and I never experienced any trouble what so ever. The baby was perfect, and great relief graced the faces of all who had been so concerned for us during the pregnancy. Since I underwent a tubule ligation while still in surgery, I longer had to worry about facing another pregnancy. The pregnancy was over, the cramps were gone forever, the nausea was silenced and a new life for our family had just begun. Now, all I had to do was recover, hopefully without suffering any set backs, and get on with enjoying raising my family again.

Not long after I was placed in my maternity room, a nurse had brought Jenae in for her first feeding. Since I was somewhat weary and drowsy from the morning's events, I decided to hand over the "first feeding" to Karen, who happily obliged. At this particular time, Karen was in great desire of having another baby herself, so she immensely enjoyed taking care of Jenae from the start. After Jenae was pleasantly plump from her feeding, she was taken back down to the nursery for some rest. While she rested in the nursery, three, little "munchkins" by the names of Jackie, Jamie and Jordan paid her a visit outside the nursery window which Karen was able to catch on video as Kathy Bell brought the excited kids to see their little, new sister. The girls were squealing and bouncing all over the nursery hallway! After they had a chance to see Jenae, then they came to see me in my room. Jackie handled all the new excitement like a champ, but Jamie and Jordan were a little concerned about all the wires and attachments that I had. I assured them that all the equipment would soon be gone and that I was fine.

That day, other visitors like Mom and Dad stopped by to see the new addition and to check on the progress that I was making. Mom and Dad were especially impressed to see how well I was doing. We have a picture of Mom holding Jenae, and as expected Mom held the new baby with all the confidence of a professional! Mom and Dad stayed for a short while, and then left to allow me to get some rest. I was doing well, and that's all they needed to feel confident about the future.

Mark remained guarded that I didn't get overwhelmed with too many visitors. He and I had both learned that from past experiences. After all the commotion had settled down a little, I had a brief moment to call Dr. RB and give him the good news. Dr. RB is a man of little emotion, but I could tell in his voice that he was greatly relieved and proud that this great feat had been accomplished. He informed me to keep him updated as I progressed through the healing process, and to call him immediately if I began to suffer from any signs of depression. I confirmed with him that he would be the first one on my list to call if such a crisis should occur. After I hung up the phone with him, it was time for the ultimate, dining experience of munching on the hospital's delectable entree that had just been placed in front of me. Of course, since I had just had surgery, my first meal consisted mostly of liquids and all the Jell-O I could eat! Whoa! What a meal! After having surgery, I enjoyed the meal despite the fact that it was mostly all liquids. Once visiting hours were over, Mark kissed me good night, and told me that he would inform the nurses to keep the baby in the nursery during the night. Mark had learned, through much experience, that I would be much better off in the morning, if I didn't have the responsibility of the baby during the night and got a good night sleep. I think he liked throwing his weight around a little bit by surprising the nurses with this order. Most normal parents insist that they do everything by the book, and in doing so, suffer the repercussions later. We had been there, wrote the book and bought the t-shirt!

I was hoping that I could fall asleep easily and sleep throughout the night, but that didn't happen. The last time that I took my trilafon was the night before I had the baby, and after that night, I was to go without any medicine until the need arose. Actually, it was the last time I would ever take trilafon for many reasons. The first one being that long term use of trilafon can result in some unwanted side effects later in life. Secondly, now that I wasn't pregnant, Dr. RB had free rein on the use of drugs that could much more accurately treat specific symptoms that might arise. Since I was now flying solo again, for the first time in nine months, I was wishing that my natural chemicals would take over and allow me to function normally, and that included sleeping without any help. I eventually did drift off to sleep, but it was a very restless sleep. I awoke during the night, hoping that I would see daylight through the hospital curtains indicating that it was morning. But, when I found the clock in my room, it clearly beamed in red, that it was only three o'clock in the morning. I tried to not let myself get too discouraged, and I continued to rest until the break of dawn. Usually, patients hate hearing all the nurses stir in the early part of the morning waking them from their slumber, but not me on this morning. I was happy that I had company with my insomnia.

We got the day started with a real breakfast this morning. I loved eating regular food again, like eggs, sausage and even drinking coffee! I know that I'm living right when I get a cup of coffee.  After that, this incredible nurse, named Carolyn, came in to change my bed sheets.  I hadn't been allowed of the bed yet, and I was still attached to many devices, so I couldn't figure out how I could move in order for Carolyn to change my sheets.  She said, honey, you just stay right there, Ms. Carolyn is going to take care of you.  The woman changed my bed sheets while I stayed in the bed!  She must have performed some kind of Houdini move because I never knew what happened.  But I did know that I wanted to take Ms. Carolyn home with me.  Later, Mark did ask her about nanny services, and she clearly stated that, outside of her hospital job, she only sat for the elderly as her side job.  Carolyn was smart.  She'd been around enough screaming babies, and she wasn't going there anymore!

Finally, a nurse came in and started unplugging me from all the foreign paraphernalia that had been attached to me for the past twenty-four hours, which offered a welcomed relief.  It proved to be one more step towards me regaining my life.  After that it was time to hit the showers! I had this one, Gestapo type nurse, that informed me that a shower was easy to do, and would make me feel much better.  I thought, "That's easy for you to say; you don't have a ten inch incision stretching across your belly eliciting pain from "sea to shining sea!"  And, let's not forget the lack of blood supply reaching my head due to major surgery and also having laid reclined for most of the previous twenty-four hours.  The many complications of surgery can create the laborious task of simply . . . taking a shower. As an end result, I did feel better, but it took a lot of effort to get me there.

The rest of the day was filled with the ritualistic duties of any day at the hospital after having a baby. Between my three meals a day, attempts to get out of bed and walk, and greetings from visitors, my day way very well occupied. Of course, I had the baby in the room with me most of the day too. Since I wasn't, presently, taking any medications, my maternal instincts and emotions had not began to surface yet. I kept waiting for all the natural hormones and general feelings of wellness to anoint me at this time of celebration, but I didn't. I had absolutely no attachment to the baby at all. To me, she was just a blob lying in her little bed. The absence of the maternal bond between mother and child left me feeling cold and heartless. Lacking this internal, phenomenal instinct, that is responsible for human survival, resonated abandonment in my mind. The baby lying next to me in her hospital bed could have been a cat or a baby. It made no difference to me. Simply put, the baby was just an object sleeping in the crib. Being robbed of my maternal fulfillment bothered me a great deal, but I stayed hopeful that soon the tide would turn in my favor leaving me free to indulge in the wonderment of motherhood. I reminded myself that things weren't all bad because, at least, I wasn't showing signs of depression . . . yet.

Late that afternoon, I was fed the early bird, dinner special, from the gourmet chef of the "La' Henry Medical Center Cafe', promptly at five o'clock in the evening. Apparently, the dinner schedule at the hospital is greatly influenced by the feeding schedule of the geriatric ward! Shortly after I finished my dinner, Karen brought the girls by to see Jenae and me. The kids and I talked all about their day and how things went at school. Each of them anxiously awaited her turn to hold Jenae, and each handled her with the utmost care and affection. I found myself trying harder and harder to concentrate on what each of them had to say. I continued to listen to the conversation and stay involved with the energetic group, but something began pulling at me, and before I knew it, I was engulfed in a cloud of isolation. No matter how hard I tried to fight off the impending doom, it incessantly grappled at my emotional state plunging me straight downward into Satan's den! Karen promptly noticed the shift in my personality and ushered the kids out of the room reconciling with them that it was their dinner time. Well, here I was again, in this old, hostile, yet, familiar situation. After a while, Mark entered the room for his afternoon visit. I told him about my symptoms, and he readily called Dr. RB. I thought, "Oh, there's no need to call the doctor; I'll just wait this one out. What was I thinking? I had a doctor with a possible cure at my fingertips, and I'm thinking that this is another hopeless predicament. I was so use to suffering, for long periods of time, without a cure, I guess, that I just supposed that this, too, would take a long time. Of course, this thought process of mine, further exemplifies the distortion of a mind under the influence of depression. Thank God for husbands like Mark! As I now, found myself sinking, faster than the Titanic, further into the abyss, I marveled at the complete, submissiveness of my mind, body and soul to this hungry predator. I remember thinking to myself several factors that ruled in my favor of overcoming the sinister depression. First, I have more experience in dealing with depression than most people. I have my faith in God, who has healed the sick and raised the dead. I have an incredibly strong will to survive, and I have an admiring and loving husband, and four beautiful children. Also, I have the best psychiatrist, who has a proven track record in accurately treating my own, severe, previous depression. I have the knowledge, the experience and the faith to fight off an attack of this kind, and, yet, I was powerless to free myself from the bondage of the depression! That's how strong and real depression is. Depression is similar to many other kinds of medical illnesses that most people relate to as physical diseases such as cancer, diabetes and heart disease. A person with cancer cannot treat the cancer by "willing" the cancer cells away. A person with diabetes can't say, "Hey pancreas, produce more insulin to metabolize the sugar that I just ate," and expect the pancreas to respond. The same response holds true for most forms of heart disease. Cholesterol is produced in the liver. People living with high cholesterol can control their high lipid count with diet, but many have to resort to medications to counteract the overproduction of cholesterol by the liver. The same holds true for depression and all mental illnesses.

Dr. RB responded quickly to Mark's urgent message, and ordered a medicine called, romadil, for me to start that night. It took a while for the hospital to process the order, but the wheels were set in motion. After an extended visit, Mark gave into his exhaustion, and I sent him home to get some rest. He was confident that with the medicine on order, that I would be fine during the night. After he left, I decided that it was the perfect opportunity for me to pull out my Bible and submerge myself in some inspirational words of wisdom. I was still fighting Goliath, but within minutes of opening the Bible, remarkably, two of my Bible Study partners, Sherry Thomason and Dana Naylor, came into the room! What are the chances? Sherry remarked at what a good student I was, and I thought, "I'm not that studious; I'm just desperate! At first, it was hard to accept company because the depression was draining my energy, but, it's always better for me to push myself forward when I have depression because it does help lift me from the mood. About halfway through their visit, I noticed that I was feeling more at ease. Slowly and progressively the dark cloud began to lift off my shoulders relieving the brunt of the oppression that had started three hours before. By the time that I started feeling better, visiting hours were over, so Sherry and Dana had to leave. They came in during the midst of a storm, and they left leaving a wake of peacefulness trailing behind them.

Just before bedtime, the nurse came in to administer my medicine. Since I was already over round one of the depression, and I fought through it without the medicine, and I was now getting help in the form of a little pill, my confidence and contentment levels raised three fold as I swallowed the pill and drifted off to sleep. I now had the internal strength of a fighter and the chemical help of modern medicine to ward off any future attacks. The medicine did help me get a much better night's sleep even though I still awoke early the next morning. As the dawn convened through the thin layer of draperies, covering the window to my room, I felt a great sense of comfort knowing that I had almost completed a full night's rest. Progressively and subtlety, things were looking up. The morning herd of nurses started their morning ritual of bombarding sleepy patients with the sound of clattering breakfast trays and a lot of "good morning" greetings. Most patients groaned at this invasive ritual, but I loved the fact that my body clock was now in rhythm with the rest of the world.

The rest of the day followed along the same path as the day before. I wrestled through with my shower still searching for that good old (and I do mean old) "Calgon take me away", experience that the Gestapo nurse so unconvincingly, raved about the day before. After I accomplished my morning tasks, I retreated to my bed for a well deserved rest. After lunch, Karen came to visit, and she and I walked down the hall for some exercise and a change of scenery. During the walk, I was horrified to spot a trail of blood flowing behind me! I panicked at the sight as I remembered the Gestapo nurse had warned me that any bleeding could mean a rupture in the incision on the bladder resulting in emergency surgery! Needless to say, I freaked! Karen calmly rushed me back to my room reassuring me that everything would be fine. Thankfully, it was a false alarm! The bleeding came from the misalignment of my sanitary pad in conjunction with my catheter. Thank God. Another surgery would have put me into a tail spin! However fortunate I was, the reality of undergoing surgery to repair an already, torn bladder hit home, as another girl, on my hall had to endure such a procedure after just having a c-section the day before! The girl's aunt, surprisingly enough, was our first next door neighbor when Mark and I moved to McDonough in 1988. The aunt's name was Coylene Higgins. Coylene had this great, maternal sense about her. You always knew that she would have warm food cooking in the kitchen, and cozy memorabilia sitting around the house. It was quite apropos for her to be taking such good care of her niece. Unbeknownst to us at that time, but that would be the last time we would see Coylene. Apparently, she had endured a bout with breast cancer, and six years later, it returned. She passed away on Christmas Eve 2004. The last people that I heard talk about Coylene Higgins, stated, "She had the faith that could move mountains." That's how I'll always remember her.

After my spastic rendition of the *English Patient* was over, things continued to move along in a positive fashion for me. That night, I encountered my usual bout of hypoglycemia that has occurred exactly forty-eight hours after every c-section that I've ever had. The first time that I experienced it, after the birth of Jackie, I was walking the halls of the hospital, and I almost passed out. The next time I suffered from it, I asked the nurses station if I could get some oxygen! After much trial and error, and a few good laughs from the nurses, I learned that I wasn't dying, but that I was simply, and momentarily hypoglycemic. Leave it up to a hypochondriac to over-react! It comes natural to me. Along the same lines as routine experiences from previous c-sections, was the "cabin fever" effect that encroached upon me every third night in the hospital. The next day, I would be released, and I was ready to go!

The day finally arrived when Jenae and I could go home. Before the doctor could release me, I had to pass a few test. The first item of business, in the morning, was the grand, ceremonious removal of the extension tube that had accompanied me since the surgery . . . the catheter. Next, I had to pass a few "ceremonious", biological tests on my own. Once I could do these things, then the doctor would sign me out, and release me back into the world. Also, Jenae was awaiting her release papers from the nursery, so that she could join me. Remarkably, she and I, both, past our tests and were ready to leave the comfort and security that the hospital had so graciously bestowed upon us over the past several days. During her stay at in the nursery, Jenae had been the absolute, model baby. Mark and I thought we might have a happy and well mannered newborn from the start. Wrong! The minute we exited the hospital, she started whaling! Mark and I were beginning to take these types of episodes, from our children, as a sign of our undesirable, parenting skills. Jackie Moddle, Mark's secretary and our dear friend, escorted us home with our new, pretty in pink, bundle, Jenae. Every step I took upon leaving the hospital, felt better than the one before. Leaving the confines of my hospital room, the hospital itself, and walking, for the first time in days, out into the great outdoors, was invigorating and liberating. The ride home on this warm and sunny, October day emulated the homecoming of a solider returning home from war. I was leaving all the struggles of the past behind me, and moving on to a life full of wonderment and endless possibilities. As we drove along the neighboring streets leading to our house, we all embraced the ambiance of the moment, realizing the significance of the struggles over the past several years and months, and, yet, not fully comprehending the full density of all the obstacles that we had tackled during such a prolonged period of time. Since the drive to our house was such a short distance, we found ourselves at home rather quickly. Mark pulled the car around the front driveway to allow a shorter distance for me to walk into the house. After he parked the car, he carried the baby, still strapped in her car seat, and started outpacing me while escorting me into the house. I squawked at him to slow down since I wasn't exactly in marathon running shape! Upon entering the house, we noticed that the kids, and their two sitters, Kathy and Karen, had taken it upon themselves to decorate the house for our homecoming. The radiant, accent of the light shining through the windows of the house, magnified and embellished the warmth and love of the artists and creators of this magnificent display. Embraced by the loving grace of our children, family, friends and our devoted, heavenly father, the healing process could commence and carry us far into a future full of promising possibilities and astonishing revelations. And, thus . . . a new dawn begins.

Chapter Seven

## Jenae -The Sequel

Needless to say, in my mind, Jenae is a miracle baby. Together, she and I encountered insurmountable odds during the arduous pregnancy, and persevered surpassing all expectations, until we reached our goal . . . victory on October 26, 1998! As we reflect on the situations that plagued this pregnancy from its inception, we must first make mention of the fact that Jenae was conceived while I was under the influence of four psychiatric medications. Next, she had to endure the ramifications from the trauma of the detoxification process that her mother underwent in order to purge her system from the harmful effects of the four psychiatric medications. After that ordeal was complete, then she suffered through the stomach virus and later, many months of sleeplessness as her mother relentlessly tried to counteract the painful effects of severe cramping. And, now, here she was, gracing the world with her petite, beautiful presence. The unexpected pregnancy and birth of this incredible, little person continues to marvel me everyday of my life. How she got here, and where she came from, are awe inspired questions that I ask myself often. She's a delightful miracle and surprise that came out of now where. Because of Jenae, I have been freed from the bondage of depression and its many demons. After a small amount of trial and error, Dr. RB found the perfect medication for me. It's called celexa, and it was recently approved by the FDA in the states just before I was placed on it. It has proved to be the perfect antidote for my symptoms. That's the only medication that I have needed since Jenae's birth, and it frees me to be myself without the drowsy side effects that I use to experience from my previous medications. Jordan had never known my true personality since I was immediately placed on those heavy medications after she was born. Once I was removed from those medicines, a new light came back into my eyes, and a new life entered my soul. In the beginning of this pregnancy, I feared the worst, and yet, ironically, not only was I spared the worst, but, graciously, I received a new life. Unbeknown to me, I had been living in bondage my entire life as I struggled with the OCD. The postpartum depression that I encountered after each pregnancy was an illuminating signal of a lifelong illness that escaped definition. Now, not only was I free from years of living with depression, but I was free from years living with OCD and it's controlling factors.

Now that I'm living a new life in good health, I've overcome every obstacle that had previously overwhelmed me with fear. A couple of years after Jenae's birth, I learned to drive on the expressway again! In fact, shortly after my first venture back onto the scenic highway of life, I propelled myself to do the unthinkable. I drove Jamie to her first audition with her modeling agency all the way to Charleston, South Carolina! I had not driven out of state since I was in College. The life force that exudes from me when it comes to taking care of my kids is just shy of amazing. After that experience, the sky was the limit, with my expectations of what I could do in this world. As you can see, I've undertaken the task of writing this book and bringing to my readers a story full of trials, tribulations and triumphs in order to share my experiences with others in hopes of building a brighter future for all. With my new lease on life, my heart and mind are open to the ever changing and growing mysteries and miracles that this life has to offer. My life is no longer stagnating and bound by fear and worry. I now embrace each day with wings of faith, and with my sights soaring! I've even taken on the responsibilities of rescuing stray animals off the streets and finding homes for them. Instead of fearing rabbis as a first thought when I see a homeless animal, I feel compassion for a helpless animal that needs a home. I'm careful to take proper precautions, with the animals that I encounter, but I better understand how to do that in a logical, educated manner. After many heartfelt attempts to rescue animals and foster and/or keep them, I am now the proud owner of two ADHD golden retrievers and one "happy go lucky" cat! Although my husband is not the animal lover that I am, he's happy to tolerate my affection for animals as long as I'm healthy. He finally has his bride back, and that's all that matters to him. My parents, "smiling Jack and fertile Ann," have their spontaneous, cheerful, blonde bombshell, darling that they can reclaim as their daughter. And my siblings have back their sister, who, in their eyes, has always "happily marched to a different drummer". My children have a mother who is alert, happy and fully capable of taking charge of the household and assisting them with their every need. Our friends walk along side with us enjoying each other's company and making new, happy memories for the future. I now live the life that I've always desired. The sun shines in my heart everyday, and as the skies return to normal after an eclipse of the sun . . . so has my smile.

## Chapter Eight

### Jamie and Jordan – Childhood OCD

"Wake up, wake up!" says Dr. Schilling. "Is she breathing?" I ask. Dr. Schilling responds, "She's just a little bit sleepy."

Later in the recovery room, Dr. Schilling enters to give me a report on the baby. Dr. Schilling states, "The baby has a problem with her breathing, and she will be taken to Egelston Children's Hospital."

"She's on oxygen, and her blood sugar is zero," says the Pediatric doctor tending to Jamie at Egelston Children's Hospital. She asks, "Can you tell us of anything unusual about the pregnancy?" I informed her about the fever that I had twenty-four hours before delivery, and then I told her that everything else with the pregnancy was fine. She said, "We can't find anything that caused her problem, but we are treating her with antibiotics." Also, she said, "The baby is requiring less oxygen, and she is improving."

A few days later, one of the nurses said, "She is out of the oxygen tent and is breathing on her own." Afterwards, she stated, "She'll just stay seven days in the hospital to finish the antibiotics."

Finally we hear from the doctor, "She's ready to go home."

That was Jamie's beginning. I believe God has a special calling for her because her journey has been unique from the start. Since her delivery, she has been a very healthy child. We have been amazed at how well she has done in school and in extra curricular activities. We were afraid that she may have lost oxygen at birth and subsequently fallen behind in her learning capacity. Quite the contrary! Jamie has surprised us all with her excellent academic success. She loves reading and learning comes easy to her. Through the great efforts of her doctors at birth, Jamie is perfectly normal. But Jamie is special in a different way because she has inherited OCD from me.

We started noticing her worry habits at the age of five. She was obsessed with the fear of dying. We talked with a pediatrician friend of our about her situation. The doctor told us that at this age, worrying about death was normal at this age, but when the worry interferes with her normal functioning, and then it is a disorder. According to Jamie's behavior, at that time, she seemed normal. However, when she entered the first grade, at age six, her teacher noticed how overly conscientious Jamie was about many things. At age seven, while I was going through my difficult pregnancy, Jamie worried herself until she couldn't eat. She lost weight, and I was terrified. She was already a skinny child before she lost weight. Many people were concerned about her as well. I took her to a pediatric gastroenterologist to have her examined. The doctor was encouraging and gave me advice about what to do for Jamie. The doctor attributed Jamie's problem to my complications during the pregnancy. After that visit, we worked on Jamie's eating habits. During this time, Jamie also exhibited what I perceive to be as panic attacks when we were away from home. I thought, "She can't be having panic attacks; She's a kid!"

At age eight, she started showing some classic symptoms of my childhood worries. She started asking the same questions that I did as a child. Examples of these questions are as follows . . . "If I touch this and put my finger in my mouth, will I die?" She washed her hands constantly and to the point of inducing skin rashes on the backs of her hands, which was a classic symptom that my siblings noticed on me at the same age. She was afraid to touch pencils because someone told her that pencil lead was poisonous. I had the same exact fears as a child. She was afraid to touch a poisonous plant just as I had been. Her childhood fears mimicked my childhood fears exactly. It was at this point, that we knew that Jamie needed professional help.

Dr. RB referred us to a pediatric psychiatrist by the name of Dr. Robert Alpern. He did find that Jamie was, indeed, suffering from OCD. He explained that OCD is caused by a lack of Serotonin in the brain. This is a disease like any other, and it has to be treated with medication. The medication of choice for Jamie, at this time, was luvox. It's been proven safe for children and very effective in treating the symptoms of this genetically, inherited illness.

During our discovery phase of Jamie's condition, she did go through some hard times. One time, I had all the children at Wal-Mart, and Jamie started having a panic attack. I dropped everything so I could embrace her and hopefully subdue the anxiety she was experiencing. I was finally able to calm her down, and we left the store. But we didn't leave without our merchandise. In our household, we may run into a few hurdles, but we always come out winning, especially when it comes to shopping. And that's the idea behind treating these types of occurrences or any other difficult predicaments life throws at us. Inflicting normalcy into abnormal situations helps create a sense of control and initiates the healing process. I've lived through enough of these types of situations to know that panic attacks and most challenges in life are, indeed . . . survivable.

Jamie is now fourteen years old and is a thriving, beautiful teenager! Her initial introduction into the world of OCD, proved to be quite challenging, but she has successfully conquered each and every obstacle. She initiated her own introduction to a modeling agency in Atlanta named Atlanta's Young Faces, by writing them a letter about herself and sending in a picture of herself. She's enjoyed a terrific career with this agency and has had many appearances on magazines covers, auditioned for numerous high profile clothing stores such as Gap, Neiman Marcus, Bloomingdales, and traveled extensively to places all over the country. As she has now entered the teenage years, her modeling stints have expectantly slowed down, but Jamie has pursued other interest such as tumbling and cheerleading. She is now starting her third year as a cheerleader at her public school, and has made the varsity squad for the second year in a row at the local high school. She is proof positive that anyone can overcome his or her obstacles in life and enjoy a great future!

Jordan, our third child, also started exhibiting some unusual behaviors at the age of eight. We assumed that Jamie would be the only one that inherited the disorder, so we were quite surprised when Jordan started showing some intriguing signs of fear. Jordan's symptoms were completely different from Jamie's and mine. Dr. Alpern originally diagnosed her with a condition called, Magical Thinking. It's a phase that children usually pass through without longevity or medication. Jordan's fears were basically that she felt that if she touched someone else's clothing, then she might turn into that person. This thought process capitulated itself into many different scenarios that didn't always fit the same pattern, but echoed the same theme. After three months of experiencing symptoms that wouldn't subside, Dr. Alpern, then decided that she, too, fit into the category of OCD. Once she began taking luvox, her condition improved greatly. After we got Jordan adjusted to the medicine and on her way to freedom from her symptoms, we discovered that she also had a slight learning disability. She, and children like her, actually are very intelligent, but they learn differently from the normal teachings of the public schools. Her diagnosis is Language Processing. It takes her longer to process information given to her in the form of instruction. In the traditional school setting, this difference in processing contributed to misunderstanding of assignments leading Jordan to frustration. Once again, when approached with a challenge, the Brittain Team always comes through. Upon much research and investigation into the problem and the corrective measures needed to solve the dilemma, we found a wonderful school in Atlanta by the name of The Howard

School. The Howard School is nationally ranked and world-renown for its ability to teach children with learning differences and prepare them for college. This is Jordan's second year there, and needless to say, she is thriving!

## Chapter Nine

### The Moral to the Story

The reason that I decided to write this book and share my story is simple. I've experienced challenges in this life like most people, but I have a different story to tell. It's my responsibility to reveal my story in order to help someone else down the road. Due to the difficulties and challenges that I endured during my time of tribulation, I became motivated to survive the unthinkable. The pain and suffering that I sustained, incited me to move beyond my boundaries and conquer my problems. As horrible as it all was, I'm thankful for the lessons that I've learned while persevering during these brutal trials. I'm a much better person today, because I have learned to face my problems directly and find the solutions. My appeal to the public in writing this book is that, my "cross to bear" in this world is similar to any difficult situation that anyone can face. I'm here to let people know that they can tackle their burdens and move onto a life that is full of promise and possibilities! To sum my belief in conveying my message to others is a quote from the Evangelist, David Ring, "I have Cerebral Palsy; what's your problem?" From here we must learn to move forward.

Epilogue

It's been sixteen years since I encountered my first panic attack, fourteen years since I first met with my Psychiatrist, Dr. RB and seven years since I delivered my last baby, Jenae. I started on this adventure with a "wing and a prayer", and encountered challenges beyond my imagination. Now, I am at the most complete stage of my life living everyday without the burden of OCD, depression, anxiety or fear. Conquering these demons has completely liberated me to be the person that I always strived to be. I'm a person free to explore life and all its wonderful mysteries while enjoying each day to the fullest! There's a saying that states, "there's no such thing as a bad day," and it's true. However empowering that statement is, it can make a person feel guilty for expressing themselves upon the encounter of such a day. My theory is this, complaining about having a bad day or complaining about anything that bothers a person is true therapy! I relish in living each day to the fullest, and in doing so, I encounter many problems. And I love to rant and rave about these problems because, to me, it means that I'm alive! It means that I have healthy emotions, and I love to celebrate those emotions! Plus, truly expressing yourself creates drama in life, and we all know that we need drama in our lives. Otherwise, why would we go to movies, watch television or read books? Everybody loves a good story!

Along with that theory, I have embraced many other marvelous ideals about life. My main goal in life is to embrace and enjoy everything that life has to offer! Climb the mountains, sail the sunny seas, love your family and lend a helping hand to those in need are my ideals in life. With this new outlook, I feel that the sky is the limit on my abilities to reach my goals! And new goals I have for myself. Since I have suffered through many years with mental and physical afflictions, I feel it my quest to help others in the same predicament. I will first succeed in helping to fund medical research for mental illnesses. Secondly, I plan on returning to college to acquire a Master's Degree in Exercise Physiology. About three years ago, I decided that I wanted to do out reach work and help people with physical and mental disabilities. That thought process has led me in the direction of Exercise Physiology. Since I already have a degree in Physical Education, and I've always enjoyed the science field, then I felt that a degree of this kind could enable me to better serve people. My goal is to work with kids from two months old to one hundred and two years old in every faucet of fitness and nutrition in effort to improve people's quality of life. Three years ago, I was fortunate enough to be appointed to the Board of Directors of the Henry County YMCA. I believe that I will enjoy a life long relationship with the YMCA and other organizations by teaching people about exercise and healthy lifestyles in effort to allow them to enjoy a life of joy and wellness. I desire to work with all types of people with all types of circumstances including adults and children with special needs, people recovering from surgeries and anyone whether they are perfectly healthy or in need of therapy. Once I discovered my true heart's desire in this area of outreach, the YMCA came along to provide me a venue in which to carry out my dreams. Among my many wishes and desires is to incorporate all types of therapy including and specializing in animal therapy. Since I'm not scared of stray animals anymore, then I have found animals to be one of the best healing medicines available. Not only that, but I have grown to love animals more than ever. I've learned about all types of animal therapy from pet therapy, which usually involves dogs and small pets, to horse therapy and even dolphin therapy. As I stated before, the sky is the limit on what can be done to help heal people in all walks of life.

Since I have become so fond of animals, I've acquired a few of my own. Over the past six years, I have brought many different dogs and cats to the house. Once again, through trial and error, we now are content with two, male Golden Retrievers named Wally and Harley, and one female cat named Hallie. I try to help animals when I see one in need, and I try to keep my husband happy in the process! Last summer, we encountered a special needs puppy that had no use of his back legs. I tried to get him help through many resources, but they all proved to be quite expensive and had no guarantee of correction. So, we ended up buying him a wheel chair in order for him to get around. We named him Zeus because I wanted him to have the name of a great and mighty warrior! And believe me; he thinks that he is one! Recently, Zeus has been placed in a special needs home for disabled animals that is located in New York. The name of the organization is Angel's Gate. You can reach them through the web at angelsgate.org. They provide an enriching and nourishing environment for special needs animals.

Not only have I grown as a person in the past seven years, but my children and family have changed and flourished too! Jackie, the oldest, is the consummate comedian always entertaining everyone she meets. She became a fantastic tennis player and competed at the State level with her High School Team at Eagles Landing. She is now nineteen and flourishing in her second year of college at Georgia State University. She loves living in the city of Atlanta, going to school and perusing internships in the political arena.

Dear, sweet, little Jamie, who started with her symptoms of OCD at the tender age of eight, is now at the fabulous age of seventeen and graduating from Eagles Landing High School this year! She has done remarkably well on the medicine luvox which she has been on since the onset of her condition. She lives totally free of all symptoms of OCD, and she thrives in her environment. She strives to reach outstanding goals that she sets for herself such as cheerleading, cheerleading and cheerleading! She's very conscientious about her abilities to keep up with the requirements of the team as well as her academic studies. Academically, she has always done well. It's amazing to me how a kid that got such a rough start in life can have every thing else turn out so easy for her. She's a natural at anything she attempts to do. Right now, she's one of the funniest and happiest teenagers that I've ever known, and we enjoy her immensely! She's anxiously looking forward to college with the hopes of attending one of the following universities, University of South Carolina, University of Georgia or Auburn.

Jordan, the other disciple of OCD, has also progressed quite well. After we diagnosed her condition and started her on the medicine luvox, she has overcome her disabilities and blossomed in return! After we got the OCD, under control, we did struggle for a while with her learning differences at school. We searched high and low for the right solutions to her challenges, and we found all the answers in The Howard School. After we researched many other schools and options, we became hopeless of finding the right place for her. But, as usual, where there's a will, there's a way. We continued our search until we landed at the Howard School, and upon entering that school for the first time, I knew it was the one for Jordan. It was incredible the peace that I found when I first walked in the door of that school. After four years at The Howard School, Jordan was accepted to Eagles Landing Christian Academy where she continues to do well. Academically, and athletically, she is soaring to new heights, and surpassing all expectations for her age. She now has her driver's license and enjoys driving herself all over town as well as to school and her sports events! She's a junior and is preparing for college!

Jenae, the sequel! What can I say about the miracle baby that saved my life? First of all, at the early age of eighteen months, a doctor looked into her eyes and said, "She understands beyond her years." And that statement about her has held true ever since that day. As I envisioned before her birth, she has always been petite and sweet. But more that that, she is curious, precocious and free spirited! Once she landed on this earth, she quickly adopted animals as her main interest. As a baby, she was always surrounded by animals since we seemed to acquire any strays that showed up. I have pictures of her eating a snack at her little table with the window open next to her. The neighbor's dog was at the window, with his head peeking inside sharing Jenae's snack with her. She's always been her own, little person. She's a tomboy in lace, and a dare devil in disguise! She explores the world with a vivid imagination, and she's content to play with her toys, all by herself, and spends endless hours doing so. She has a best friend, Breanna, who remarkably almost shared the same birthday two years apart. The uniqueness about their friendship is that Breanna and her Mom, Sheree, came to visit us one day when Jenae was just four months old. Something Breanna did made baby Jenae cackle out loud! Not only is it unusual for a baby of that age to laugh out loud, but it's especially strange for her to do it in loud tone. She and Breanna have had a common bond ever since that time. There's not a doubt in my mind, that God had a special reason for bringing Jenae into our lives, and for that reason alone, I deem her the true miracle baby. It's bewildering to me, as I ponder this extraordinary, little creature that I carried her into this world, yet she's the one that gave life to me. She is now ten years old, and has a great passion for horses and most recently, cheerleading. She's on a local competition squad where we all get to travel often to watch her perform. It's the perfect arena for her to show off her joyous smile!

And now for the grand, conductor who held us all together through all the conflict and turmoil, my husband, Mark, has impressively handled all the debilitating years and lived to tell about it. He was my knight in shinning armor saving me from the evils of this world and stopping at nothing until the job was accomplished. He had the ability to take control of every situation that hit our family and make something good come out of it. He had no idea what he was getting into when he married me, and although it's been a rough ride, he wouldn't have it any other way. We've recently talked with each other about what were the main attractions that we had for each other when we each knew that to other was the one to marry. He said about me, that he wanted to be married to someone who was fun. Hopefully, I've fulfilled that roll and will continue to do so. As far as having fun during the difficult years, all I can say is that, at least, I'm not boring! Today, Mark is doing better than ever. He has instrumentally helped to build the law firm from a small, yet cozy, office building located on the busy street Keys Ferry in the heart of McDonough, Georgia to four, rather large office buildings dispersed throughout Henry, Butts and Spalding Counties! What use to be a handful of lawyers with a limited supply of secretaries, is now a conglomeration of twenty lawyers and over one hundred supply staff! Mark is an investment, business man and real estate lawyer maintaining a credible reputation among his colleagues and business associates. Thankfully, he and I are in a place now where can enjoy the fruits of our labor and relish in the delight of our children. We now find ourselves in much reflective and introspective thought about the world, our family and how we have achieved our happiness. Oh, and last but not least . . . I would be remiss if I didn't mention Mark's quest to have a baby boy. He's thought about what it would be like to have a son, but then he realized that God has done the best that he could by giving him the only, male successors that he'll ever need . . .Wally and Harley.

The End

www.ingramcontent.com/pod-product-compliance
Lightning Source LLC
Chambersburg PA
CBHW080538170426
43195CB00016B/2602